Edited by
the Dresden Frauenkirche
Foundation

on the occasion
of the consecration
of the Frauenkirche
on 30th Oktober 2005

Andreas Friedrich (Text)
Jörg Schöner (Photos)
Rosemarie Nitschke (Translation)

THE FRAUENKIRCHE
IN DRESDEN
History and Rebuilding

Michel Sandstein Verlag

Inhalt

page 9
The Fascination
of the Frauenkirche –
an introduction

page 13
Early history, ideas and
planning stages for building
a new church

page 23
Life and work of the
master builder George Bähr

page 29
The new building of the
Frauenkirche 1726 –1743

page 41
Shape, iconography and
pictorial decoration

page 51
The importance of the
building in the church and
in society

page 59
Constructional repairs,
alterations and restoration
over a period of 200 years

INHALT

page 65
Destruction, treatment of the ruin, efforts towards rebuilding

page 75
Early history and planning preparation for the rebuilding

page 87
The years of rebuilding

page 117
Specific features of the rebuilding – a monument and its active use

page 127
New life in the Frauenkirche

page 130
Sources of literature and illustrations

page 132
Chronology of the history of the Frauenkirche

The Fascination of the Frauenkirche – an introduction

The consecration of the Frauenkirche on October 30th 2005 is the completion of unique teamwork of high symbolic power and worldwide influence. The extraordinary achievement of rebuilding this baroque domed church authentically after the almost total destruction in World War II is sometimes called the "Dresden Miracle". The scientific and technological perfection, the craftsmen's skills and the artistic quality in reconstructing this famous architectural monument are probably unparalleled, however the actual miracle consists in the fact that the construction of this church succeeded in appealing to so many people and in attracting their attention.

high into the sky went around the world and touched people deeply. It was a reminder of the magnificent German contribution to world culture, which once was made and, at the same time, of the outrageous criminal nature of a war instigated by Nazi Germany, the effect of which now hit this place with a dreadful force. The ruins in the heart of the devastated city soon became a memorial place of high emotional influence, and became even more so, the further the rebuilding of Dresden progressed all around, in accordance with the new principles of socialist town planning. It remained a stumbling block and a constant reminder that with the domed building

Why did such a strong fascination emanate from this project? How can we explain the fact that a small impetus – the "Call from Dresden" coming from 14 citizens in 1990 – gained such dynamic force to direct the interest and strong support of thousands of people all over the world to this building task? A major reason for this undreamed-of echo probably lies in the specific history of this building. The masterly creation of George Bähr and his workmen is considered to be the highlight of Saxon baroque architecture and to all intents and purposes the ideal of a Lutheran civic church. Through two centuries it was a place for the proclamation of the reformatory faith, high-ranking church music and the living history of the town. The picture of the destroyed House of God with the remains of a staircase tower and the choir apse rising accusingly

of the Frauenkirche, the crown of the townscape, had been destroyed. Many people harboured the hope that this gaping wound in the Dresden townscape would finally be closed and with this the scars of the unfortunate period in German history, still within them, could heal. But above all the call for peace, understanding and reconciliation among peoples emanated from the ruin and again and again brought together people of the Christian motivated Peace Movement of the GDR to this place during the years of the global armament race after 1982. In striving for peace, justice and preservation of creation Dresden citizens organized political resistance which led to the peaceful turn of events in Eastern Germany and enabled the reunification of Germany. The spirit of that time was expressed in the "Call from Dresden" which was sent out into the world

Fig. 1: Ruin of the Frauenkirche with the overturned Luther monument

Figs. 2, 3: In quiet memory with candles at the ruin

Fig. 4:
Frauenkirche construction site, Handing over of the "Flame of Reconciliation" by guests from the town of Gostyn (Poland), 16th April 1999

Fig. 5:
In 1988 Dr. phil. Fritz Büttner founded in Remagen-Oberwinter the first society for the rebuilding of the Frauenkirche which financed, amongst other things, the set of bells for the Frauenkirche

Fig. 6:
Professor Günter Blobel hands over his donation from the Nobel prize for Medicine to Volker Kreß

Fig. 7:
Volker Dümmler collects donations in front of the Munich Frauenkirche for the Dresden Frauenkirche – day by day whatever the weather

Fig. 8:
Silversmith Allan Smith from London, son of a British bomber pilot, working on the orb for the Frauenkirche cross, 23rd October 1998

Fig. 9:
Young joiner preparing the wing of a portal for the Frauenkirche

not knowing that it would have such an unforeseen effect. The great spiritual resonance and financial support given to the rebuilding project in the whole of Germany made the Frauenkirche a symbol of brotherhood and hope for the growth of inner unity, for a renewed community of Germans in a unified Europe. People of all age groups, different origins and world views and many nations committed themselves to this joint task for the most diverse personal reasons, made modest or large contributions to the rebuilding fund and carried forward the idea of reconciliation. For many of them it was their own life story which connected them with the town, this church or its influence on art and music. However, the impulse for the rebuilding, once begun, reached far beyond and with each recovered piece of rubble and with each newly positioned stone the interest and readiness of the people from near and far to help was growing. The public discussions on principles and partial problems of rebuilding aroused the attention of many people and motivated them to become involved in the debate and support the fascinating project. Besides individuals, more and more circles of friends and sponsor groups, firms and institutions committed themselves to the church building. Stonemasons and sculptors from all over Germany worked on ashlars free of charge following the plans of the construction team and young joiners made portals and inner doors for their final qualifying piece of work. Over 600 concerts for the rebuilding of the church given by the musicians under Professor Ludwig Güttler and many other ensembles carried the enthusiasm for this great task into the world and motivated countless listeners to make spontaneous donations or to join the sponsor group. A substantial part of the building cost came from private sources by means of Donors' Certificates of the Dresdner Bank, the selling of watches for the Frauenkirche and many other imaginative schemes. The media ensured that the construction work as well as the religious services and concerts in the growing church were covered in the news which had a widespread effect. The stream of effective support grew in width and depth and really gained strength by connecting people from different countries. It led to the great event of the consecration of the church which represents a gratefully celebrated conclusion of 14 years of construction work and the prelude to a new life in the rebuilt House of God, the Frauenkirche.

Fig. 10: Performance of the "Messiah" on 10th December 2000. Virtuosi Saxoniae under Ludwig Güttler and the Hallenser Madrigalisten

Fig. 11: Moritz Bodenehr: The old Dresden Frauenkirche seen from the south. Graves of the Frauenkirche cemetery in the foreground, the Materni hospital on the right, copperplate engraving, before 1720.

Early history, ideas and planning stages for building a new church

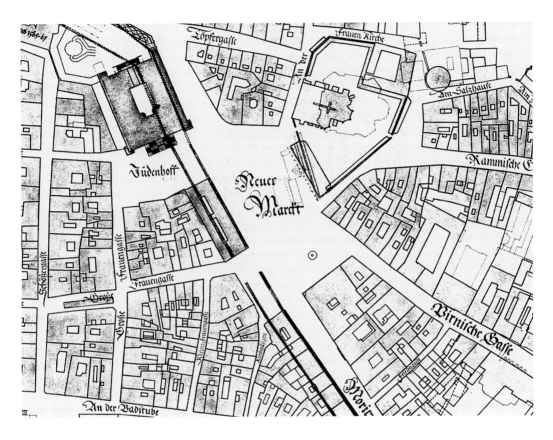

The oldest settlement of Dresden appeared in the Early Middle Ages on the left bank of the Elbe river as a small fishing village on a flood-free area. Here, at the crossing of important trade routes near an Elbe ford, a church had been erected as early as 1000, which was called "Unser Lieben Frauen" (Our Blessed Lady). It was the spiritual centre of a large parish which included the surrounding villages of the Elbe valley with a prevailing Sorb population.

It remained the main parish church of the town even after a planned urban settlement of Merchants had been established in the area of today's Altmarkt. The first Kreuzkirche (Church of the Holy Cross) which had been built in this place around 1216 and had originally been consecrated as a church dedicated to St. Nicholas – the patron of the merchants – only gained larger importance in Dresden church life around 1400. The old Frauenkirche in the middle of the only existing town cemetery at that time was altered at the end of the 14th century creating a three-nave Gothic hall church out of a previous Romanesque church.

During the following 100 years a long choir with side chapel, a ridge turret with bell frame and a late Gothic two-floor sacristy annex were added (Fig. 11). The rapid growth of the town and dependent rural settlements soon led to a shortage of space in the church. This was the reason that galleries were inserted after the Reformation and visitors to the church service had to be placed under the roof around an opening in the ceiling so that they could listen.

Fig. 12: Plan of the suburb around the Frauenkirche (Neumarkt area) with medieval town wall, as it was in 1721, extract from Heinrich Koch, drawing 1935: The Neu-Dresden fortress

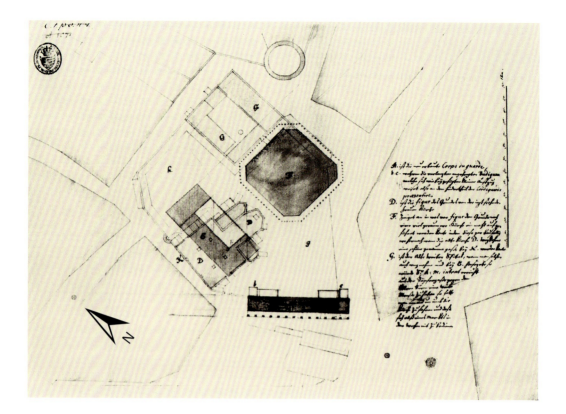

Fig. 13: Johann Christoph Naumann:
Plan for the reshaping of the Neumarkt 1717/18

A. newly erected Hauptwache (main guardhouse)
b. c. small stalls behind the main guardhouse
D. ground plan of existing old Frauenkirche
F. planned new church
G. Materni hospital to be removed

The more rural suburb in which the Frauenkirche was situated remained cut off from the town centre by the town wall until the first extension of the town and the re-planning of the Dresden fortress under the Electors Moritz and Augustus in the middle of the 16th century (Fig. 12). Only the pulling down of the old wall at the Frauentor enabled the architectural reorganization along Moritzstrasse and at the "Neuer Markt", with the most important public buildings being the Royal Stables (1586–1591) and the old Cloth Hall (after 1591). The new houses of the middle-class citizens at the Neumarkt were in most cases built with the eaves having the same height and often with dormer windows in the gables as well as decorative oriels copied from the rich choice of Renaissance forms.

The baroque reshaping of the civic town around 1700 gradually took place within the framework of the irregular medieval ground plan of the town. The architectural intentions of the Electoral court aimed, however, at creating a square of generous proportions especially in the area of the Neumarkt. This was the reason why in 1715 a new main guardhouse was built by Johann Rudolph Fäsch which had its well-proportioned facade facing the Neumarkt and at the same time concealed the ugly mixture of buildings around the Frauenkirche and cemetery. At the same time Johann Christoph Naumann developed, on behalf of the main building authorities, a project for the reshaping of the cemetery of the Frauenkirche and the Neumarkt taking into account the architectural ideas of Augustus the Strong and developing them further. As far as the Frauenkirche was concerned, a new building on a square ground plan east of the medieval building was planned (Fig. 13). For a long time the Elector had demanded the abandonment of the old burial ground in the densely populated city area. He planned to have large-scale alterations to buildings for the arsenal and the powder tower and entrusted this task to the French architect Zacharias Longuelene.

It seemed that the time was ripe for major considerations concerning the future of the old Frauenkirche because the vaults, supporting columns and roof turret showed serious damage requiring large-scale safety measures. Besides that the old church building became more and more inadequate for divine services. When, in Spring 1722, parts of the building had to be closed and the roof turret had to be pulled down it was high time to act. The Town Council together with the municipal master carpenter George Bähr and later the chief master builder for Saxony Johann Christoph Knöffel inspected, by order of the Electoral Governor Count August Christoph von Wackerbarth, possible building sites for a new building beside the old church. It was assumed that the old church would be used as long as possible and that the medieval Materni hospital would remain untouched.

The first plans for a new Frauenkirche were submitted by George Bähr in May 1722 and showed a ground plan in the form of a Greek cross with a semi-circular choir. They made clear from the very beginning of the planning that the required size of the new building would not work without the demolition of the hospital buildings if other prerequisites had to be met, such as keeping free the view from Neumarkt to the powder tower and the arsenal. It also became clear that the construction of the new building could be started beside the old church which was still in use but that the complete demolition of the old building would soon become unavoidable. Therefore the building commission consisting of representatives from the town and the Church Consistory – inaugurated in September 1722 – again demanded a reduction in the size of the building and the cost, which according to a first estimate given by Bähr and the municipal master mason Johann Gottfried Fehre amounted to 103 075 talers. The citizens of Dresden could not raise this sum and requests for financial subsidy were repeatedly rejected by the Elector. As a result of this the plans and definite building preparations were suspended; only the moving of the graves to the Johannis Cemetery was pursued. Demarcation of the proposed ground plan on the cemetery was carried out for the first time in August 1723 and again showed the conflicts with the existing old buildings.

The preliminary project suggested by George Bähr, on which the cost estimate and the demarcation of the ground were based, has been handed down only incompletely. It follows the earlier ground plan of the Greek cross and envis-

Fig. 15: Frauenkirche, Preliminary Project by George Bähr, Probably 1722/24, south view, reconstruction attempt from ground plans of the preliminary project and façade of the "First Project" 1724/25, drawing Dieter Schölzel

ages an octagonal interior being surrounded by three jutting galleries. A semi-circular choir is added to the eastern arm of the cross and staircases are positioned in front of the other arms. Eight slender pillars carry a flat cloister vault enabling light to come from above into the centre of the church through a central round opening (Fig. 14). A drum floor with windows is arranged above it and was meant to be crowned by a bulbous dome with lantern. A roof turret with bell cage rises above the bulbous roof of the chancel. With this design Bähr further developed his own building ideas, which had already marked his previous church projects in Schmiedeberg (1713–1716), Beitsch (1716–1719) and Forchheim (1719–1726). However, the much larger central building in the capital was given a more splendid monumental appearance (Fig. 15). In the idea of space and the staggered axial arrangement of pulpit, baptismal font, altar and organ Bähr follows the contemporary theological principles for the building of Protestant churches as defined in the writings of Leonhardt Christoph Sturm between 1712 and 1718. The pulpit jutting out from the choir screen into the centre like a ship's bow moves the preaching of the Word very vividly into the centre of the Lutheran service (Fig. 16). The pews on the ground floor are concentrically brought into line with this position. Baptism takes place behind on another slightly raised central area within the

Fig. 14: Frauenkirche, Preliminary Project by George Bähr, 1722/23, horizontal section at vault level

view of the community. The high importance of church music in Protestantism at that time becomes clear by the arrangement of three organs and galleries for the singers at the sides above the altar area within the pillared choir space. A crypt floor is positioned under the whole building and a hole exists in the centre of the church for lowering coffins when burying the dead. The earnings from the burial fees were seen as an important source of finance for the new church building.

All subsequent intermediate stages for planning the Frauenkirche show that Bähr stuck to the programme of use and the stylistic and liturgical basic principles of his first building plans.

It was not until July 1724 that the patrons of the church and the town expressed their views on the plans and cost estimate from 1723. Bähr was asked to reduce by half the building costs and the dimensions of the building and to position it so that the services in the old Frauenkirche could be held for as long as possible. Subsequently the master builder developed several versions with a reduced ground plan and other changes which were meant to improve the layout of the church and reduce the building costs. The widened altar area connected to the central space was the result of the decision that the gallery staircases flanking the choir area should be abandoned and of the more elegant curving of the galleries at the choir crossing. This led to an axial lengthening of the dimensional effect (Fig. 17). The pillars forming an octagon carry an octagonal flat vaulted inner cupola getting daylight through dormer windows in the curved base of the cupola. Another octagonal space which also gets light through dormer windows in the wooden top of the cupola, from which "heavenly music" may sound and which could hold more listeners, is situated above a central opening in the inner cupola (Fig. 18). This idea probably goes back to examples which can be seen in chapels in palaces of that period (Weimar, Wolfenbüttel and others) or in courtly houses with large stairwells, ball rooms or summer-houses. Moreover this type of space for visitors had existed in the old church in the loft above the main church although there it represented only a makeshift solution.

Bähr subdivides the exterior of the building by columns and Romanesque windows rising above the windowless base. The strong main cornice running round the building is topped off above the entrances in the main axes by segmental arch gables with cartouche. The loft area arranged above with a row of windows for the top gallery floor has been inset out of the main line by means of inwardly curving buttresses. This leads up over the concave base of the roof above a strongly profiled eaves cornice to stone flame vases positioned at the corners.

The octagonal main cupola rises above a strongly-featured string-course and already forms at the base the bell shape which in the future would be the main feature of the church (Fig. 20). Bähr positions very decoratively the strongly profiled lantern with a carillon on the cupola and also designs the bell tower above the chancel with a baroque extravagance of forms. The curved roof has three levels of dormer windows which also give a lively decorative effect.

This draft served as basis for a new laying out of the ground plan in summer 1724 which, however, did not satisfy the Electoral building authorities, because the requirements of urban

Fig. 16: Frauenkirche, project by George Bähr, intermediate stage between Preliminary Project and "First Project", probably 1723/24, horizontal section at level of 1st gallery

Fig. 17: Frauenkirche, preliminary stage of "First Project" by George Bähr, probably 1724/25, ground plan 1st gallery

Fig. 18: Frauenkirche "First Project" by George Bähr, 1724/25, north-south section

Fig. 19: Frauenkirche, project by Johann Christoph Knöffel, 1725, north-south view

development with respect to a reshaping of the arsenal area were again not adhered to. The authorities criticized the functional solution as well as the architectural design of the building. Count Wackerbarth complained, for instance, about the limited capacity of the staircases, the meagre incidence of light into the main area and the unfavourable relationship between building volume and usable space. But above all Bähr's building design did not correspond with the modern architectural taste prevailing at the court which was strongly influenced by early French Classicism. This more severe academic classical style had already influenced the drafts made by Longuelune and Knöffel for new secular buildings of this period like the arsenal complex or the knights' academy in the Neustadt. This style was meant to be applied also to the new church building in the capital. The chief councillor of the Consistory, Löscher, speaking on behalf of the church, expressed his discomfort concerning the size and splendour of the building which seemed to be inappropriate for a Protestant House of God. Bähr went over the plans again several times, had the site marked out again in November 1724 and organised the purchase of sandstone, lime and structural timber in conjunction with the participating craftsmen. The Town Council had, in the meantime, approved the amended plans but – because of fresh objections brought forward by the chief building authorities – the project was not accepted by the director Count Wackerbarth.

In 1725 he finally commissioned the young state master builder Knöffel to draw up a counterproposal to Bähr's plan in order to find a way out of the deadlock. This approach to have competing designs for important building tasks from different architects was common practice in the building authorities of the court and in most cases led to a very fruitful blend of different ideas and to a conclusive overall solution. In this case, however, the Council as an independent, civic authority commissioning the building was presented with an alternative plan by a court architect trying to implement the ideas of the sovereign. In retrospect we can say that even in this case decisive factors in the successful completion of the building came from the competition between different ideas. In November 1725 Knöffel presented his design together with a model showing that the building had a square ground plan and was more densely organised and thereby took better into account the relationships between Neumarkt and the arsenal complex than Bähr's plans had done. Knöffel suggests a circular central space with eight enormous radially arranged pillars carrying a higher inner cupola (Fig. 22), which, just as in Bähr's proposal, gets light through the dormer windows and is connected with an inserted drum floor by a round opening lined by a circular colonnade. The basic idea of a Greek cross in the ground plan had been abandoned but the distance between the pillars in the central space is wider in the main axes. In spite of this the con-

Fig. 20: Frauenkriche, "First Project" by George Bähr, 1724/25, south view

Fig. 21: Frauenkirche, project by Johann Christoph Knöffel, 1725, south view

nection between the longer and barrel-vaulted choir and the main space seems to be quite constricted (Fig. 19). Beside the choir there are two sacristies and small winding staircases leading to the galleries are installed in the corners of the building. Completely different from Bähr's proposal is the design of a main west façade with a broad flight of external stairs and two flanking towers containing the staircases for the galleries and carrying the bell cages. There is, therefore, no bell tower above the chancel. In Bähr's proposal the outer cupola has a curved base starting directly above the main cornice. The windows for giving light to the third gallery have an oval form and are integrated in the arrangement of the colossal pilasters of the window fronts. This makes for a more severe, vertically oriented façade structure compared with Bähr's design and has a more drily academic effect (Fig. 21). Formal considerations for the exterior design are obviously of prime importance for Knöffel, whereas the liturgical requirements of the Protestant service in the arrangement of the pews, the position of the pulpit, organ and choirs are given less consideration.

This counterproject by Knöffel did not find unanimous agreement either on the Council, the Church Consistory side or by director Wackerbarth, but the injection of new ideas revived the planning process. Bähr was instructed to make a wooden model in accordance with Knöffel's plans, which was "examined" by the main building authorities in March 1726. He provided for discussion a second model which expressed his own ideas. New decisions were taken in this meeting showing the way forward for further planning. It was especially recommended to have towers on all four corners of the central building to obtain almost the same grand effect towards all sides of the town. For the same reason the outer cupola should "better be brought up higher" in an oval

Fig. 22: Frauenkirche, project by Johann Christoph Knöffel, 1725, ground plan ground floor

Fig. 23: Frauenkirche, Second Project of the chief building authorities, 1726, south view

Fig. 24: Frauenkirche, Approbation Proposal by George Bähr, 1726, south view

form. Changes concerning windows, galleries and "Betstübchen" (private prayer boxes) should bring more light into the interior. The choir should be opened wider to the interior and made more simple by installing only pilasters. The circularly arranged enormous pillars of the cupola were to go directly from the galleries to support the vertical orientation of the central space towards the cupola. New plans were prepared on this basis by the chief building authorities and in the office of the municipal master carpenter in the Spring of 1726. With the four diagonally positioned staircases at the corners and the large dormer windows in the base of the cupola they come quite near to the final shape of the building (Fig. 23). The sketches show a mixture of classical elements from the Knöffel draft and motifs of Bähr's style, however in the plans handed in by Bähr for approval by the Council in May 1726 his abundance of forms is the determining feature. The ground plans (Fig. 25) and sections show the tendency towards simplification and restriction to essentials, not only because of the required cost reduction but probably also to make it easier to obtain the "approbation" of the chief building authorities. There had been a vehement dispute at the beginning of this planning stage between the Council and Count Wackerbarth because the town was dissatisfied with the building delays and counter-projects of the royal building authorities. Time was pressing to start with the building because the preparation work had made progress and the disrepair of the old Frauenkirche was becoming more and more a risk.

George Bähr's plan for approval represents a unique synthesis of different approaches in a planning history lasting more than four years. He provides the corner towers with a concave base for the main cupola and equips them with gables and short vases (Fig. 24). The slightly parabolic superelevated cupola is meant to have a wood

Fig. 25: Frauenkirche, Approbation Proposal by George Bähr, 1726, ground plan 1st gallery

Fig. 26: Frauenkirche, Approbation Proposal by George Bähr, 1726, west-east section

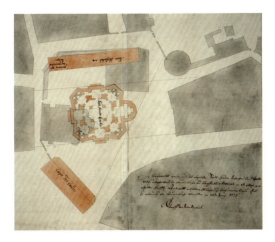

Fig. 27: Frauenkirche, Approbation Proposal by George Bähr, 1726, layout with ground plan of the crypt floor, extract

The round building north-east of the Frauenkirche is the Powder Tower. West of the new building we find the ground plan of the old Frauenkirche indicated in grey. Indicated in red are the guard house to the south-west and a new building of the Materni hospital to the north.

ment expressed by the royal court. In the prime position near the bend of the river he conceives a monumental domed building which Augustus the Strong had been dreaming of for his residence on the Elbe river for a long time, thinking of the Venetian example of the Grand Canal with Santa Maria della Salute. It did not take long for the governor to give his approval and the approbation was issued on 26th June 1726. One month later the building was finally marked out and the excavation work started in the area of the chancel. On 26th August the ceremonial laying of the foundation stone took place in the presence of many notables and allegedly 10 000 spectators with a commemorative sermon delivered by superintendent Valentin Ernst Löscher and a jubilee Cantata by the choirmaster-organist of the Kreuzkirche Theodor Christlieb Reinhold. For this occasion the Dresden Council had a commemorative medal struck in silver and gold. It shows the south view of the church according to Bähr's second draft (Fig. 28).

construction with a copper roof, whereas it is recommended that the curved cupola base will be covered with special cost-saving stone slabs. The lantern above the cupola will be topped by an obelisk to acknowledge the royal sovereign and promoter of the building. The chancel would have a concave wooden roof framework with copper cover. The zone of the main cornice is stretched wider to accommodate additional windows in the frieze for the third gallery floor. Front gables are positioned above the projecting middle part of the building to accentuate the main axes. They are provided with an oval window in each of them to let additional light into the upper area of the church. A special feature of this central building is that public entrances of almost the same standard are situated on all sides and at the four staircase towers.

The plan shows that, once again, there are slender pillars in the interior (Fig. 25/26). At this stage there exist no curved arrangement of the pews as well as no choir screen with the side stairs and the central pulpit as it existed in the original plan; the organ is shown on the north gallery of the choir. These acknowledgements to Knöffel's draft seem to be preliminary tactical concessions to the sanctioning authorities. They will be removed later during construction.

In the layout plan with the incorporation of the crypt floor which Count Wackerbarth wanted to have additionally, Bähr indicates explicitly that the view from Neumarkt to the powder tower near the arsenal will be kept clear and that a new building will be possible for the Materni hospital (Fig. 27). This makes clear that the architect is trying to fulfil all requirements for urban develop-

Fig. 28:
Memorial medal
for the laying of the
Frauenkirchefoundation stone,
Johann Wilhelm Hoeckner,
1726

Life and work of the master builder George Bähr

During his lifetime George Bähr was highly esteemed and accepted and his fame may even have become greater in the course of rebuilding his grand Dresden Frauenkirche in the present day; however little is known about the course of his life and what he was like as a man. This can easily be explained in view of his humble origins and initial social position as a craftsman during the age of absolutism. The personality and work of similarly famous contemporaries in courtly services are in most cases far better documented. Therefore it becomes all the more interesting to track down the stages of his life.

George Bähr was born as the son of Andreas Bähr, a carpenter, in Fürstenwalde/Osterzgebirge on 15th March 1666 and died at the age of 72 in Dresden on 16th March 1738 before the building of the Frauenkirche was completed. His grave was to be found in the Johannis Cemetery outside the Pirnaisches Tor town gate until this cemetery was abandoned; the stone tomb (Fig. 29) and the urn with the remains from the grave were then moved to the crypt floor of the Frauenkirche.

Little is known about the period from his birth until his appointment with the Dresden building authorities on 20th October 1705. It is certain that Bähr received a qualification as carpenter and organ builder and worked as a journeyman for several years. Organ fronts made by him are said to have reached Florence. There are good reasons to assume that the young carpenter took part in the building of the village church in Carlsfeld/Erzgebirge (1684–1688) according to plans by Wolf Caspar von Klengel, because this remarkable building had obviously served as a pattern for later church designs made by Bähr (Fig. 30). It is known that shortly after this, George Bähr's presence in Dresden was for the first time documented in 1689 and again in 1693. It is said that he had also studied mechanical sciences and was gifted in all kinds of work. It is therefore no surprise that the Dresden Town Council swore in the almost forty year old Bähr as municipal master carpenter, although at this time he was not yet in possession of his master's certificate. He was

Fig. 30: Carlsfeld, Trinitatis Church, probably Wolf Caspar Klengel, 1684–1688

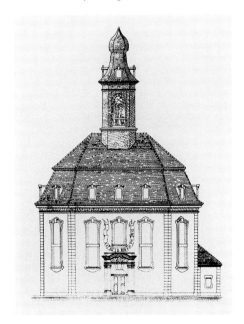

Fig. 29: Frauenkirche, tombstone of George Bähr in the undercroft after restoration, 1996

Fig. 31: Church in Dresden-Loschwitz, built 1705–1708, Elbe side

Fig. 32: Dresden, George Bähr's dwelling house, An der Mauer, remodelled by George Bähr 1711, demolished 1911, photograph 1910

appointed because he was said "to know more than a mere master carpenter" and to be "a man of high scientific knowledge". Together with the municipal master mason Johann Fehre the Elder he was immediately entrusted with all tasks of the building guilds working under the Town Council. They included the building supervisory boards of the town responsible for all civic and municipal buildings, the churches and cemeteries, road building, water supply and disposal, all facilities of town hygiene and health precautions and more. The building rules laid down in Dresden very early in 1713, 1720 and 1736 formed the basis of such governmental obligations and adherence to them was additionally supervised by the chief electoral building authorities. Although his job was not well paid, the appointment represented a kind of monopoly to receive orders for the planning and building of many municipal and civic buildings and together with Fehre he fulfilled the task very successfully and gained wealth and public recognition. For all that, the master carpenter probably seldom had the ultimate say in the design and architecture of the facades, which at that time lay in the hands of the masons' guild. It may well be that his cooperation in the building of the remarkable Loschwitz Church (1705–1708, with J. Fehre, the Elder) was limited to creating the roof framework and the wooden equipment of the galleries (Fig. 31).

In 1711 he bought a town house (An der Mauer 2/corner Seestraße) and redesigned it for the needs of his growing family (Fig. 32). Bähr set up a drawing studio with large windows in the attic for himself and his fellow-workers. In the exterior design of his own house he could show his own style as an architect, which for his time showed somewhat conservative, old-fashioned features and reveals its origin in the carpenter-like decorations of the panels and flat carvings in doors and portals. Bähr was, for the first time, the author of a design on a large scale for the project of a palace in Sorau (Zary) in Lower Silesia around 1710 in which he also clearly refers to stimuli from a plan by Karcher and Pöppelmann for the Dresden Palace. A bit later Bähr designed one of his first original new church buildings in Beitsch (Biecz)/Lower Silesia between 1716 and 1719 ordered by a noble patron (Fig. 33).

Fig. 33: Beitsch (Biecz)/Lower Silesia, church from north-east, 1999

Fig. 34: Schmiedeberg, Church of the Holy Trinity, exterior from north-west

Just as in the new parish church in Schmiedeberg (1712–1716) Bähr designed a central building on the basis of the Greek cross with high windows, steep roof and a roof turret on top. Attempts at this had already been made in the Carlsfeld church (Fig. 34). As an ideal combination of the main parts of the Protestant service we have in most cases a "Kanzelaltar" (altar with pulpit above) and in front of it a baptismal font close to the congregation which gathered on angled rows of benches around the liturgical event. A richly decorated organ front forms the highlight of altar architecture in the churches of Schmiedeberg and Forchheim (1719–1726) which he built together with Johann Gottfried Fehre the Younger (Fig. 35).

The common features of all these rural churches designed by Bähr are the several galleries running around, which have a space-forming function but are installed in the building like furniture and are carried by plain wooden supports without special tectonic subdivision. In general George Bähr treats the classical architectural canon in quite a free and unconventional way compared with the master builders at the court. He puts the functional requirements of the preaching service for as large a number of listeners as possible at the centre of his design. A lot of practical experience from the planning of earlier small church buildings went into the long process of shaping the Dresden Frauenkirche in addition to the ideas and design rules of contemporary theoreticians on church building like Leonhard Christoph Sturm. With the Frauenkirche Bähr designed a grand and artistically greatly enriched synthesis of very different intellectual approaches and formal suggestions on a far larger scale and became a clever figure of integrating influence in the large working community of builders and artists. Not least Bähr acted also as a kind of general entrepreneur in today's meaning of the word.

The planning and building of the Frauenkirche kept the mature and experienced master builder busy from about 1720 until the end of his life and numerous other municipal office obligations constantly claimed his full attention and energy. In addition to this he had to deal with building tasks in the town and a whole series of church buildings and palace projects in the more distant surroundings. Bähr designed a grand front for the new Silbermann organ in the Sophienkirche between 1719 and 1720, which became the prototype for many other organs from Silbermann's and many other workshops and also influenced the architecture of the organ front in the Frauenkirche (Fig. 36). After 1722 Bähr supervised the reshaping of the palace in Seußlitz for Count Heinrich von Bünau in which the chapel was equipped with the characteristic design elements of the master builder as there are several galleries, boxes for the patrons, a "Kanzelaltar" and organ gallery and the slate-covered roof turret with baroque top (Fig. 37).

On various occasions Bähr could implement his ideas together with Fehre the Younger when fires had damaged churches as, for instance, the town church in Königstein (1720–1724). Again and again he tried to give the original hall buildings

with their Gothic style a more centred character by equipping them with galleries round the edge and comprehensively conceived "Kanzelaltar". This is shown in the outer appearance of the churches in Kesselsdorf (1723–1726) and Schmannewitz (1732–1739) underlining the polygonally designed chancel by strong octagonal choir towers with bulbous top and lantern which – seen from the east – give the impression of central buildings (Fig. 38). In this way he had also planned to reshape the town church in Hohnstein (1724–1728); this was in the end done only incompletely and in an oversimplified way. On behalf of Count Adam Friedrich von Flemming George Bähr supervised the rebuilding of the burnt down Hermsdorf Palace (1729–1732) in a simple baroque form. Here the boldly curved top of the middle tower with a polygonal spire – consisting entirely of stone – catches the eye and appears to be a practical exercise for the cupola of the Frauenkirche.

The last large municipal building task which was carried out parallel to the vaulting of the Frauenkirche by Bähr and Fehre the Younger was the completion of the Dreikönigskirche in Dresden Neustadt (1732–1739). It had been planned by royal order in the course of the remodelling of Altendresden into a "New King's Town" by Matthäus Daniel Pöppelmann as a three-nave hall. Bähr's main responsibility was the huge loft roof construction and the substantially changed design of the interior in which the double gallery system enclosed the oval space for a total of 3 000 participants in the service (changed at the rebuilding).

Because of his illness which began in 1736 and gradual loss of strength, George Bähr could do only little to complete his great life's work. He died in 1738 before completion of the cupola of the Frauenkirche with its slender lantern. He left six children from his third marriage; his widow married Bähr's cousin Johann George Schmidt in the same year. He had been Bähr's pupil and successor and his work was influenced by his master long after his death.

Fig. 35: Schmiedeberg, Church of the Holy Trinity, interior, George Bähr 1712–1716, photograph 1965

Fig. 36: Dresden, Sophienkirche, front for the Silbermann organ, unknown draughtsman acc. to design by George Bähr 1719–1720

Fig. 37: Diesbar-Seußlitz, palace church, interior with alta, pulpit and organ, after 1722

Fig. 38: Kesselsdorf, village church, exterior from south, remodelled by George Bähr 1723–1726

Fig. 39:
Old Frauenkirche and laying the foundation
of the new baroque building, view from the north
in 1727, copperplate engraving
by Moritz Bodenehr, 1738

Fig. 40, page 29:
Frauenkirche, condition of building work in December
1727, isometric presentation by Torsten Remus, 1995

a Materni hospital
b wall surrounding the cemetery
   with roofed tombs in front of it
c half-timbered house used as orderly room
   with roofed lime pit
d charnel-house
e temporary bell tower for the bells removed from
   the church tower already in 1722
f remains of the previous church
g the "New Frauenkirche under construction
   at basement level

The new building of the Frauenkirche 1726–1743

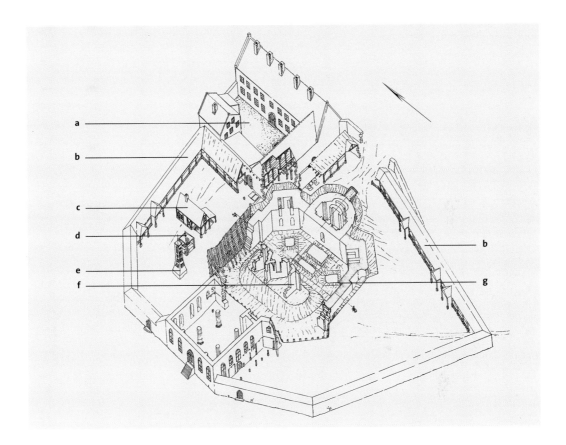

Extensive building preparations and purchase of materials, the marking out of the ground plan and the excavation for the chancel had been carried out before the laying of the foundation stone on 26th August 1726. The mighty foundations and the crypt floor required a foundation depth of 12½ ells and therefore the southwest corner of the Materni hospital had to be pulled down immediately for safety reasons and the adjoining parts of the building had to be prepared for further use. The masonry of the foundation consisting of sandstone ashlars was laid as the soil was excavated and – advised by the municipal master mason Johann Gottfried Fehre – with generous dimensions to carry the big loads of the cupola and the towers. The walls of the cellar under the chancel were completed by the end of 1726 and the ground for the eastern half of the exterior walls was excavated. (Fig. 39). Now the choir of the old Frauenkirche had to be removed to enable further foundation work for the western part of the church. The last service was held on 9th February 1727. The Gothic choir was pulled down within a short time and the excavation was speedily extended to the west. By August 1727 the exterior walls of the lower floor and the pillar foundations were completed. Further demolition work was carried out step by step depending on how many workmen and horse-drawn vehicles were not needed for the new church building. Usable stones from the demolition were re-used for backing the walls as was also done with many stones recovered during archaeological rubble clearance between 1993 and 1994. By 1727 the total stonework of the foundation with the substructure of the eight pillars in the interior was completed up to terrain level and the exterior base with the base moulding could be positioned. The first shaped stones had to be ready for this. They were prepared under the supervision of master Daniel Ebhardt in the stonemasons' shed on the Neustadt Elbe meadows. New plans probably did exist for this, because the pillar bases were already made some-

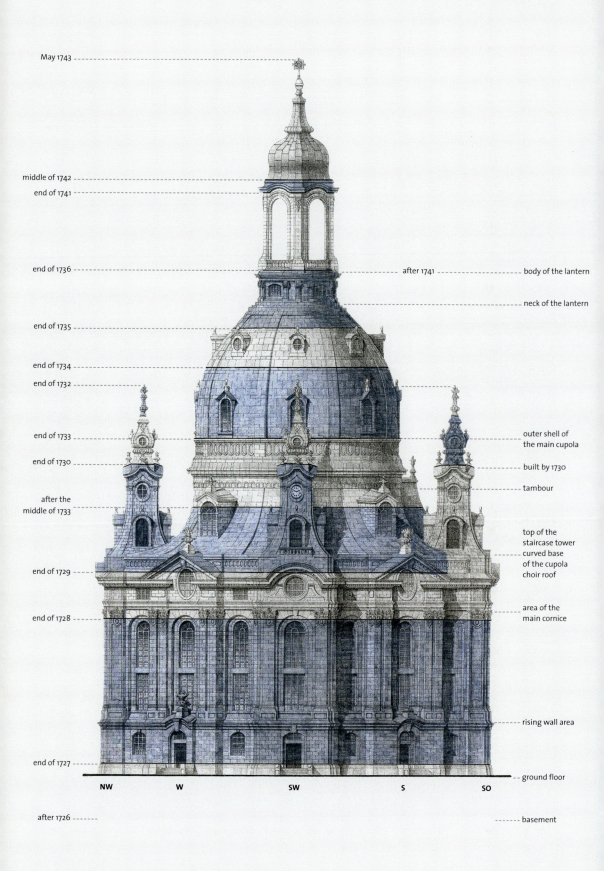

Fig. 41:
View of the Dresden Frauenkirche with indication of the horizontal sections of the building and the annual building sections

what stronger than planned in the Approbation Proposal. The completed system of the basement floor is clearly shown in the reconstruction drawing by Remus (Fig. 40). The sketch of the Greek cross within the square of the exterior building with the enclosed circle of the eight pillars in the interior is here closely connected with the idea of offering for sale as many crypt spaces as possible between the load-bearing ashlars of the wall and of making them accessible from two octagonal circular passages. It was also intended to subdivide the cross-shaped main cellar for use as burial chambers, whereas the choir cellar should be used for church equipment. The crypt cellars lying diagonally received a barrel vault in 1728 and the first burial took place in November of the same year (Fig. 42).

During the progress of the erection of the exterior walls, the staircases and the pillars special care was taken to see that the building grew evenly to avoid different loads on the foundations. The revised plans emphasized new features and brought back earlier design ideas for the interior. As a result of this the diagonal entrance axes of the staircases in the exterior building were additionally accentuated by segmental running around, and above the dynamic graduation of the curving galleries and the solemn rising of the slender pillars with the projecting half-pillars up to the inner cupola enrich the effect of the church interior to an extraordinary degree. The original liturgical design with the central pulpit rising out of the choir screen and the concentric arrangement of the pews, the flights of stairs rising to the altar area at the sides and the main organ above the altar front remains the basis for the spatial perception (Fig. 43). The sculptor Johann Christian Feige became more and more involved in the decorative design of the interior after 1729. His wealth of ideas and creative power were a fortunate addition to the shaping of the building by George Bähr as the chief architect. Many documents from the building period give evidence of the intensive and fruitful cooperation of the guild masters Fehre, Ebhardt and Feige with Bähr. They took part in the decision-making for the shaping of the cupola and the corner towers, which were re-designed after the main cornice area was completed in December 1729.

The rapidly growing building cost represented an urgent problem for the Council and the Church

arches in the main cornice and with this the upper ending of the wall took on a more vivid form (Fig. 44). Bähr's integral baroque spatial perception becomes still clearer with the revised design of the interior. The further widening of the choir, the inclusion of a floor for the "Betstübchen" (private prayer boxes) with the window ribbon

Consistory. The initially approved total building sum of about 83 000 talers was spent by 1729. The income from a Christmas lottery in 1727, from collections, the selling of burial chambers in the crypt vaults and from a lottery for preferred box seats in the so-called "Betstübchen" (private prayer boxes) did not meet expectations. The hope for

Fig. 42: Frauenkirche, ground plan of the crypt floor, copperplate engraving by Christian PhilippLindemann, 1734

Fig. 43: Ground plan of the first gallery floor, copperplate engraving by Christian Philipp Lindemann, 1736

larger subsidies from the court concerning concessions for the supply of stones and for wages were not fulfilled. As a result of this the main cupola, originally planned with wood and a copper cover, had to be replaced by a cheaper solution. In September 1729 Bähr suggested making at least the base of the cupola of solid stone. For this he developed detailed proposals for the making of the joints and water drainage to counter the rising objections of the building commission and the municipal master mason Fehre who was responsible for the positioning of the stones. Bähr pointed out before the Council that the loads from the inner cupola and the stone base of the roof would be safely absorbed by the system of staircase towers, pillars and

Fig. 44: Frauenkirche, diagonal view from southwest, unknown draughtsman, around 1729/30

wall projections. It may be taken for granted that during this time he considered building the outer cupola totally of stone. The master stonemason Ebhardt also presented plans and cost calculations for a stone cupola, but the completion of the church interior by the inner cupola was more urgent.

Revising the whole appearance of the building, Bähr made a proposal in Spring 1730. It foresaw the rising of the four staircase towers by 17 1/2 ells to 31 1/2 ells and the enrichment of the curved tower tops with sculptured decorations. This shows that the master builder intended to make the exterior of the building look higher and to have more sculptured details decorating it. The changed plans convinced the building commission to provide the finances in spite of all objections and stonemason Ebhardt received the order to build the corner towers and the neck of the cupola as well as the chancel roof in stone.

The work on these structural parts could be carried out at the same time as the vaulting of the inner cupola took place. The smoke and flame vases for crowning the staircase towers and the frontispieces were manufactured in the workshop of the sculptor Feige who had already made the pilaster capitals, and the gallery consoles as well as the capitals of the half pillars and pilasters in the interior. The carpenters worked in the interior of the church installing the galleries. The third gallery was interrupted in the main axes and led to the large arched windows with concave sweeps to allow more light to come in. A small fourth gallery was installed above receiving light from the oval windows in the gable triangles. This change meant a new enrichment of the baroque concept of space by the intersection of the enveloping shells and by emphasizing the cross form of the ground plan. This is characteristic of the long and complicated process to find the final shape for this building.

Influences on the development of shape and technological solutions resulted quite naturally from the teamwork of the master builders but also from input from the Council and the Church Consistory as patrons or even from the Royal Court. At first this came through the Higher Building Authorities but as the building rose Augustus the Strong took a more and more personal interest in the work's progress. The King himself received architect Bähr in audience at least five times – for the first time in August 1731 – and expressed suggestions and wishes for changes. He showed a special interest in the magnificent effect the domed building would have on the town silhouette and even considered having the recently erected main guardhouse on Neumarkt pulled down. The open-mindedness of the sovereign towards the civic building project in his residential town encouraged the Council to ask several times for a substantial contribution – be it a donation of copper for covering the cupola or a financial donation. However, the hoped for positive answer did not arrive and, thus, the Council let the King know that the erection of the outer cupola had had to be postponed and that all resources would be concentrated on the completion of the interior so as to be able to use the church in the

Fig. 45: Frauenkirche, west to east section through the choir, drawing by George Bähr (?), around 1731/32

near future. In Spring 1732 the substructure of the ground floor was filled in and the floor slabs could be laid after the vaulting of the large cross-shaped crypt had been finished. After that the whole interior was again covered with scaffolding to carry out stuccowork in the inner cupola, on the pillars and gallery balustrades and to start the painting of the interior. After long negotiations concerning cost and specification of the organ the order for its construction was given to Gottfried Silbermann in Freiberg in November 1732. In the meantime George Bähr had worked out detailed plans for the equipment of the choir which included – beside the organ front – the whole altar retable, the side rooms as well as the choir balustrade with the central pulpit, the confessional boxes and the flanking staircases (Fig. 45). A competition was advertised for the sculptural design of the altar front in April 1733 in which the court sculptors Johann Benjamin Thomae and Johann Christian Feige as well as the stonemason Daniel Ebhardt took part. The subject dictated by the Dresden Town Council was "The story of Christ on the Mount of Olives" and the drawings and elaborately designed model by Feige obviously attracted the patrons and experts in a most convincing way (Fig. 46). George Bähr bought Feige's model, offered the Council to do the complete job and obtained the general contract for all furnishings in the area of the chancel in December 1733.

As a matter of course Bähr made Feige and his workshop partners in the sculptural design.

The pulpit, the choir balustrade and the two confessional boxes in the front area were completed by the time the church was consecrated on 28th February 1734. At the instigation of superintendent Valentin Ernst Löscher regular church services took place on Saturdays and Sundays from this time on. However, this made the ongoing work in the interior more difficult.

The death of Augustus the Strong on 1st February 1733 in Warsaw represented a big turning-point for the country's policy as well as for the construction work in the residential town. His son and successor – elector Frederick Augustus II – appreciated art very highly and the Town Council hoped for support for the ambitious building project. The Council asked Bähr, Fehre and Ebhardt once more to hand in comparative cost estimates for the outer cupola designed in wood or stone and presented these documents to the Elector with the wish to promote the building of the cupola. He decided to use all the money – 28 366 talers – collected in support of the Protestant Salzburg emigrants in Saxony for the Frauenkirche building.

Fig. 47: Frauenkirche, section, view and ground plan of a stone cupola, draft by George Bähr, around 1733

Fig. 46: Frauenkirche, drawing of altar and organ front (here with the sacrifice of Isaac), drawing by Johann Christian Feige, 1733

Fig. 48: Frauenkirche, draft of a cupola by an unknown draughtsman, cross section and horizontal section with a ring anchor, probably 1734

Fig. 49: Frauenkirche, diagonal view (with colonnade in the space of the cupola), copperplate engraving by Christoph Philipp Lindemann, 1735

Fig. 50: Frauenkirche, diagonal view (with a vertical masonry ring above the curved cupola base), copperplate engraving by Christian Philipp Lindemann, 1734

This instruction was very much disputed but it gave a noticeable impulse to the continuation of the building work. Bähr became more and more inclined to have a stone cupola and gave as reasons for this before the Council cost advantages and the grand effect in which the church would emerge as a mighty mass of stone – "one single stone from top to bottom". This idea had been developing in him for a long time, been reflected in new plans since 1730 and seemed to him possible as far as building technology was concerned because the constructional prerequisites had been created when building the substructure (Fig. 47). The municipal master mason Fehre and members of the Council raised serious objections concerning the stability of the cupola. Bähr was able to counter these critical objections by providing new cost estimates and expert opinions on the load-carrying capacity of the structural system. He pointed out the ingeniously planned "pyramidal" flow of forces from the cupola via the flying buttresses under the curved cupola base and via the arch-supported wall sections connecting the main pillars with the staircase towers, projecting walls and exterior walls down to the precautionary well-dimensioned foundation walls. In addition the interior pillars – in any case consisting of the best stones – are not exposed to excess loads. Probably Bähr also took into consideration building experience available in Saxony concerning load distribution in Gothic pilaster churches. The design of the cupola may well be based on examples from Italy like the cathedral in Florence or Santa Maria della Salute in Venice, which were known to the experts from copper engravings. Bähr, however, finds his own incomparable solution for the realisation of his building idea. He makes the cupola steeper, not including the classical drum floor, forming it by two massive shells connected by inner ribs. A spiral passage exists between the two shells. The voluminously rising bell is crowned by a slender lantern topped off by a high-rising open-worked obelisk (Fig. 49).

The Council handed over the new plans and expert opinions to the new general director of the Chief Building Authorities, Jean de Bodt, for judgement and approval. In August 1733 he gave his positive opinion on the stone cupola together with the recommendation to provide the cupola with circular reinforcement consisting of forged iron and to make the lantern much lighter as a wooden construction (Fig. 48). This was the basis on which the Town Council concluded a contract with George Bähr on 31st August 1733 for building a stone cupola within 13 months(!) amounting to a total contract sum of 19 000 talers which soon turned out to be well short of what was needed. Bähr's repeated requests for additional money were always rejected by the Council so that the master builder had to use his own resources to finance the building of the cupola during his last working years. The actual work on the cupola only started in 1734 according to revised plans, which show that Bähr stretched the building by installing a vertical wall ring with a decorative facing balustrade above the final cornice of the cupola base. Only by doing this did the cupola get its characteristic elegant, bell-shaped sweep

(Fig. 41/50). These new deviations from the approved project caused de Bodt to express severe criticism during an inspection of the site in August 1734 but Bähr could sufficiently justify them in a statement before the Council. He said that the iron ring anchor was far better to be installed in this expanse of the wall, that the higher and somewhat enlarged windows would let more light into the cupola space and that the curving of the cupola would be preserved. This made it possible for the outer cupola to be curved and completed within two years, including the neck of the lantern. The substructure of the lantern was built higher than designed in the first plans and was provided with four windows in addition to the upper ring opening effectively to increase the incidence of light from above into the inner eye of the cupola. Thereby the spatial perception with the solemn gradual rising of the central building with the light flooding into it was realised.

During the building of the cupola the furnishing of the interior was completed because with the completion of the inner cupola there was a

Fig. 52: Frauenkirche, draft by David Schatz (completion of the lantern neck by a platform), copperplate engraving by Christian Philipp Lindemann, 1739

Fig. 51: Frauenkirche, draft B for the lantern, drawing probably by Johann Christoph Knöffel, 1738

temporary closure of the interior. Giovanni Battista Grone from Venice worked as theatre painter at the court and produced eight paintings between the stuccoed belts of the inner cupola. They represent the four Evangelists with their typical characteristics and the spiritual virtues of faith, love, hope and mercy as allegoric figures. The lower circular gallery of the inner cupola was provided with an artistically forged and painted railing. The altar front was installed by the stonemason Ebhardt at first architecturally to allow the completion of the organ gallery and the organ case including the sculptural work, the painting and gilding work. Silbermann had constantly urged for this to be finished to complete his own work. The magnificent organ with 43 registers was accepted by renowned experts in November 1736 and festively consecrated. The new instrument was especially honoured with a concert given by Johann Sebastian Bach on the occasion of his appointment as court composer on 1st December 1736.

The sculptural work on the altar figures in the workshop of Feige lasted almost another two years and in July 1738 the excellent result was attested by the court sculptor Benjamin Thomae. George Bähr had died after a long, severe illness on 16th March 1738 and did not live to see the completion of his work.

This was especially relevant for the completion of the outer cupola because first cracks in the arches and pillars under the inner cupola had already appeared during the vaulting work in 1736, for which the master builder was called to

account. In 1737 the Council demanded expert opinions from various sides and temporarily postponed the erection of the lantern. A statement from the architects of the Higher Building Authorities, in which Bähr's higher and heavier cupola was criticised and in which the demolition of the stone base of the lantern was recommended, was presented to the general director de Bodt in May 1738. A light-weight wooden lantern with a copper or lead cover was to be chosen. Another expert opinion by Gaetano Chiaveri went as far as to demand the complete demolition of the outer cupola and its replacement by an elegant wooden construction. The municipal building commission did not want to have to deal with this advice and asked the renowned master builder David Schatz from Leipzig to give his expert opinion on the condition of the building. He inspected it very thoroughly and recommended the preservation of the cupola, a professional repair of all damage which had appeared and doing without the lantern. He pleaded for a viewing platform with balustrade on the lantern base, which was advocated by the Elector and King (Fig. 52).

The Dresden Town Council regarded Schatz's opinion very positively and had his proposal of an "observatory" and two models of a lantern made as wooden models – even in coloured versions – in situ on top of the cupola. The results, however, were not satisfactory from an aesthetic point of view and the Council tried to obtain more suitable proposals for a rising but light-weight lantern top for the cupola. Fehre and Knöffel handed in their proposals to be decided upon by the King at the end of 1739. Knöffel's elegant draft (Fig. 51) came near to Bähr's earlier drafts with the obelisk-type top but Frederick Augustus II decided to have the more compact form of Fehre's proposal with a double bulbous dome (Fig. 53). Astonishingly, again a stone construction was planned and ordered from Fehre and the new master carpenter George Friedrich Winkler, Bähr's successor on the supervisory board. The difficult and dangerous work in building the lantern at a great height lasted from 1740 to 1743.

In the meantime the design of the altar including the colour design and gilding work by sculptor Feige and the scene painter Stephan Gabriel Batlowsky was completed. The isolated arrangement of the pulpit in the middle axes was acoustically unsatisfactory in the church services and in 1738 its installation at the northwest choir pillar on a higher level was decided upon. Feige began with the re-installation including the manufacturing of a new sounding board and a new staircase for the pulpit as well as the building of a lower lectern in place of the middle pulpit (Fig. 181). It seemed that his change necessitated decoration of an area above the altar mensa previously covered by the pulpit. Feige solved this problem by creating a relief with the three spiritual virtues and a consecration inscription of the Town Council (Fig. 56).

On the 27th May, 1743 building work on the Frauenkirche was formally completed by the final positioning of the gilded orb and cross which radiated far into the distance.

Fig. 53: Bernardo Belotto, called Canaletto (1721–80), The Neumarkt seen from the Jüdenhof (extract)

Shape, iconography and pictorial decoration

The Dresden Frauenkirche represents in its uniqueness a complete representation of baroque building work in Germany and a high point in Protestant church building and – at the same time – the culmination of George Bähr's work as an architect. Influences from contemporary European art are combined with typical elements of Protestant baroque church buildings which, especially in the Saxon cultural area, are determined by the Lutheran concept of faith and divine service.

The building in its entirety can be regarded as the preaching of the Lutheran faith in stone, as had been intended by its creators. George Bähr's project took up important ideas contained in the drafts of the younger state master builder Johann Christoph Knöffel. It was theologically confirmed and interpreted mainly by superintendent Valentin Ernst Löscher as a member of the municipal building commission. The ingenious work of the guild masters and artists, cooperating under the supervision of George Bähr, developed into a great and godly teamwork until the highest peak – in relation to the shape and furnishing of the building – was achieved. Especially the municipal master mason Johann Gottfried Fehre, the sculptor Johann Christian Feige, the master mason Daniel Ebhardt, the painter Christoph Wehnert, the scene painter Stephan Gabriel Batlowsky, the court painter Giovanni Battista Grone and the Freiberg organ builder Gottfried Silbermann enriched the building with their own contributions.

The fascinating shape of the building is derived from George Bähr's original idea which comes from his earlier church projects in Saxony and from other model buildings of the Protestant tradition. The building is based on the form of the cross which already exists in the crypt floor and is more strongly expressed in the church interior by accentuating the main axes with a longitudinal orientation to the chancel and is underlined on the exterior by the central projections which are topped off by the frontispieces. The interior of the central building is characterised by the cupola-carrying circle of pillars soaring magnificently into the staggered cupolas. The figure of the cross is once more repeated in the diagonal line of the ground plan connecting the staircase towers with each other, which from the outside, in the form of corner towers like sentinels, rise up with the mighty dome. The form of the cross and the circle are integrated in the square of the ground plan which is based not only on town-planning considerations. Bähr and the theoreticians on church building of that time saw in the central building the ideal form for the Christian community gathered around God's Word. Hence it seems as if the fusion of the completely geo-

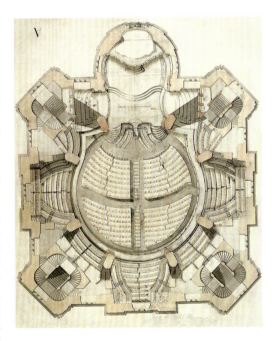

metrical figures of circle and square with the symbol of the cross represent the image of divine perfection under the sign of salvation, i.e. preaching of the Word in a building. The lapidary large shape of the building appears as firm as a rock against the waves of time, "a stronghold of faith" and "a strong tower" as it is often said in the language of Reformation hymns which is rich in imagery. The richly sculptured building combines monumentality with a certain weightlessness of the curved base of the cupola, secure ties with

Fig. 54: Frauenkirche, overall view from south-west, end of the 19th century

Fig. 55: Frauenkirche, seating plan (ground plan third and fourth galleries), drawing by George Bähr, around 1734

the ground combined with a soaring up into the sky. The entirely "nonclassical" and "noncatholic", not at all triumphant form of the cupola top represents the symbol for a congregation sheltered under a roof while the flame vases topping the building in many places stand as signs of the burning love and pious worship of God (Fig. 54).

Uniting forces of quiet composure act simultaneously on the visitor to divine service under the central cupola in the interior and, together with those of a dramatic perception of space, have an exalting emotional effect. The entire baroque design power of the master builder based on the religious happening in the church is shown in the play with space, the mingling of horizontal and vertical movement in the constructional elements, in the creation of ambiguous spatial structures and shells merging into one another and the concentration on the centre of the House of God, as well as the altar, as the point of liturgical and artistic culmination of the building. Churches are – as superintendent Löscher said in his consecration speech on 28th February 1734 – "Auditoria, where people come together to hear God's Word and take the Holy Sacraments", but no "Theatra" to see "vain presentations and large processions". However, this church interior, which is not just a modest prayer hall, has something prestigious and theatrical about it.

The raised choir space with its arrangement on three levels in front of the altar and the choir balustrade is very richly and splendidly designed and stands out from the central space for the congregation as a special place. It acts in this way as a stage for the liturgical happening and the music performance in the divine service by the organ and choirs. At the same time it is not only reserved for the clergy in accordance with Protestant concepts. It is accessible to all for baptism, receiving the Holy Sacrament or wedding ceremonies. It was a long time before the main parts of Protestant divine service consisting of Word, Sacrament and Music were so united in such a definitive composition. The preaching of the Word from the pulpit is at the centre of the service and the pulpit has found its place at the intersection between the circular nave of the church and the choir oval. Like a ship's bow it projects into the space for the congregation and the preaching from the pulpit should give direction, proclaim God's love, call for repentance and give consolation (Fig. 56/180). Two confessional boxes are situated at the side of the pulpit and integrated in the architecture of the choir screen to underline that a proper preaching sermon should lead to self-examination, confession and forgiveness, which is confirmed in receiving the Holy Sacrament. Two more confessional boxes are positioned on both sides of the altar near the place of the sacrament. The teaching element of the sermon is made clear by the fact that additional benches as a "place for examination" could be positioned directly in front of the pulpit on which young people came together for a talk with the priest on faith and Christian lifestyle. This was a place for permanent public pastoral guidance. For acoustic reasons the pulpit was moved to the northeast pillar in the interior by sculptor Feige in 1739 and replaced by a lower lectern for readings and catechism examinations. The congregation remained in their concentric seating oriented to the original place where the pulpit had been. It was important that as many seats as

possible within hearing distance and with a good view were available as can be seen in Bähr's plans for the allocation of church seats (Fig. 55).

The central building is also a spiritual image of the close community of believers gathering in prayer and singing, to listen to the Gospel, see each other and feel closeness. The space which stretches to all sides is light-flooded, not only for easy seeing and reading of hymnals and devotional books, but also as a sign of the shining of God's word as it was often described in contemporary sermons and hymns. The sculptural decoration of the interior supports the spiritual message of the building. Cherubs with four wings are positioned in the capitals of the pillars. They surround the space protectively and invite the congregation to join in the angels' praise of God

Fig. 56: Frauenkirche, altar and choir balustrade with lectern, 1939

Fig. 57: Frauenkirche, angel with trombone on the organ front

Fig. 58: Frauenkirche, inner cupola with paintings of the four evangelists and the Christian virtues Faith, Love, Hope and Mercy by Giovanni Battista Grone, reconstruction by Christoph Wetzel, 2004

Fig. 59: Painting in the cupola showing the evangelist Matthew

The cheerful splendour of the interior directs the view upwards into the inner cupola in which the pictorial statements are repeated in new forms. The harmony of inner pillars and transverse arches is continued in the cupola by stucco lesenas. The richly sculptured decorations show leaves, blossoms, plant rosettes and freely carved festoons. Pictures with stuccoed framing are arranged between the lesenas showing the four Evangelists alternating with the allegories of the Christian virtues of faith, love, hope and mercy (Fig. 58). These ceiling paintings are the work of Giovanni Battista Grone from Venice who received great recognition as a court painter and theatre designer. In these paintings he does not revel in illusionist representation of the sky full of figures. He keeps strictly to the design programme in individual fields on special subjects taken from Italian domed churches. Grone's mastery becomes

(Fig. 61). Foliage, festoons and ornaments point to the beauty of the universe, the power within plants and the expectation that the proclamation of the Gospel may yield fruit in the hearts of the listeners. The stuccoing and the beautifully marbled pillars, arcades and the gallery balustrade surrounding the interior indicate the splendour of a temple in the final heavenly Jerusalem, whose ornaments and precious stones are often praised in baroque poetry and music. Besides the bright yellow colour in the whole interior the colours blue, red and green are dominant. Löscher connects these colours (already in his speech on the occasion of the laying of the foundation stone in 1726) with the Christian virtues of faith, love and hope: "the beautiful sky-blue so pleasing to the eye of faith, the exquisite green keeping alive our hope, the sweet red, in which pure love is glowing".

Fig. 60: Painting in the cupola "Faith", above in the roundel the parable of the importunate friend

Fig. 61: Pier capital with Cherub, coloured version as test section for reconstruction

visible by this restriction when he represents the Evangelists as full of life and differentiates between them in relationship to their work and its creation. Instead of a large theatre he stages small scenes giving Matthew an angel pointing to a document from the Old Testament as the basis of the Gospel. He has the Evangelist Mark listening to the roaring of the lion which the prophets compared to the mighty voice of God. Luke is leaning thoughtfully on the bull, symbolizing Jesus' sacrificial death. John with the eagle – reminding us of Christ's Ascension – is absent-mindedly looking upwards. The figures allow us to assume that the large fresco paintings by Michelangelo in the Sistine Chapel may have served as an example, however they are the artist's own invention (Fig. 60). The oval paintings, of the godly

virtues arranged between the Evangelists, follow entirely the traditional iconographic Canon showing the female figure of "fides" (faith) with the cross and sacramental cup (Fig. 59), "caritas" (love) amongst three children and with a burning heart in her hand and "spes" (hope) with an anchor shining in a heavenly beam of light. Grone adds to these female figures a fourth figure "misericordia" (mercy) throwing a coin to a poor man and thus reminding the onlooker that, especially in a town of well-to-do citizens, shared Christian responsibility for the poor should be observed. Hence the central space for the congregation is elevated spiritually by the paintings in the cupola and makes clear that Christians are gathered here visibly under God's Word. When praying together "hearts are uplifted" as it says in a gospel of the Holy Sacrament. The upper space of the cupola was made for the sole purpose that music could come down from the "higher choirs" to the whole congregation at prayer. Grone's paintings all show that a clear blue sky is shining on the figures and daylight is pouring through the openings in the cupola on to the entire splendour of the interior and finally down to the gathered congregation. "The heavens are open, where one can hear God's Word and where people believe, love, hope and show mercy" [Münchow].

The whole altar is seen as the high point of the spatial design and the centre of the "sermon in a building" within the domed building. Its shape and sculptural design were developed during a long process of discovery and design. The architectonic subdivision already existed in the first project by George Bähr in 1722 and was varied several times until its final shape was reached by Bähr in 1733 in a main model showing a uniform altar and organ front. The proposed iconographic programme for a centrally arranged altar relief contained at first the birth of Jesus, Christ's Resurrection or Ascension and the sacrifice of Isaac (Fig. 46). Finally the Dresden Town Council specified the subject "The Story of Christ on the Mount of Olives". Bähr entrusted Feige with the sculptural work, whereas Ebhardt obtained the contract for the stonework of the altar wall. Feige tells the story of Christ praying in the Garden of Gethsemane when kneeling on a cliff and receiving strength from God's answer delivered by an angel coming down head first out of a cloud holding a cup (Fig. 62/65). The sleeping disciples Peter, James and John are made smaller in perspective while in the background in front of the city of Jerusalem the traitor Judas steps through the town gate at the head of a group of henchmen.

Jesus and the angels as main figures in dramatic movement are fully sculptured and the abundant vegetation in the garden is depicted in a very life-like way whereas the remaining scenery is carved as a flat relief. Over the whole sculpture there appears a cross-shaped aureole of clouds with angels' heads and with God's eye in the central symbolic triangle (Fig. 64); a ring of golden rays hovers behind it. This is to indicate that the three-in-one nature of God is always present and that God wants to be near His Son in the hour of

fear when even His friends are sleeping. An angel comes down from the divine aureole indicating Christ's passion by carrying a cross.

This biblical scene goes back to the Late Gothic iconographic traditions under the name "God's Need" and has been similarly shown in Passion paintings by Dürer and Cranach the Elder. Altar sculptures in the area of Saxony have probably been influenced by the altar of the Trinity Church in Görlitz by Caspar Gottlob von Rodewitz (1713). Sacred depictions of this type are deeply rooted in Protestant devotion in Saxony relating to the Passion and are widespread in baroque times while the contemplation of Christ's suffering is also typical of baroque Passion music. The representation of Jesus' fatal hour with

Fig. 62: Altar, total view, after restoration 2005
Fig. 63: Face of a Cherub on the organ front
Fig. 64: Aureole with God's eye above the altar relief

the indication of the act of salvation on the cross shown in the area of the altar is meant to strengthen the faith of clergy and believers receiving the Holy Sacrament and, of course, also the entire congregation.

Together with the sculptured decoration of the altar front consisting of garlands with ears of corn and grapes, the entire altar is an indication of the sacrificial death and the gifts of grace – Christ's flesh and blood in the form of bread and wine received in the Holy Sacrament. The joyous yet sombre pillar architecture of the background with the Communion ambulatory behind the altar mensa between the two doors serves as a backdrop for the liturgical happening of the Holy Sacrament. The lower area ends in a richly decorated angulated base cornice. On top it has two found above the doors for the communicants: on the left Paul with the book of the Gospel and with a sword reminding us of his martyr's death, on the right Philip with the cross-shaped baptist's stick indicating his missionary work and later crucifixion. A relief table is set in the centre above the altar showing again the Christian virtues as the allegoric figures of faith, love and hope which are named in a consecration inscription of the Dresden Town Council as spiritual guidance for the "building" citizens.

The entire altar receives a triumphant almost musical intensification over the soaring gable by the magnificently decorated organ front subdivided also into three (Fig. 191). The famous, many-voiced work by Gottfried Silbermann is kept in a precious shrine, whose sculptured decorations

Fig. 66: Moses with the Tablets of the Law and the Apostle Paul with the sword

Fig. 67: Aaron and the Apostle Philip with the cross

decorative vases with corn ears and grapes as well as four large fully sculptured figures being related to Confession, Holy Sacrament and Baptism. The figure of Moses seated on the left with the Law Tablets recalls the Old Union of God with the people and the guiding power of His commandments. The right-hand figure with a similar pose representing Aaron with the censer is an indication of priestly service in the temple (Fig. 66/67). The Apostles of the New Testament are to be and gilding work were made in Feige's workshop. It is positioned to demonstrate the entire polyphony of baroque church music. Two angels with trombones are sitting on the top cornice indicating the announcement of the Last Judgement (Fig. 57). The cornice ends with several sweeps in a cartouche of clouds in which the letters S. D. G. – Soli Deo Gloria – are inscribed dedicating the entire architectural and artistic work of this church to the glory of God alone (Fig. 176).

Fig. 65: Detail of the altar. The praying Christ is given strength by an angel. In the background the silhouette of Jerusalem and the gate through which Judas and the soldiers enter the garden of Gethsemane. Christ shows clearly visible traces of destruction and restoration.

Fig. 68: Front page of the preaching sermon on the occasion of the laying of the foundation stone for the Frauenkirche given by Valentin Ernst Löscher, 1726

The importance of the building in the church and in society

The erection of the Frauenkirche at that time was a self-conscious and demonstrative act by the Protestant citizens of Dresden. The general religious-political situation in Saxony had substantially changed by the Elector's – Frederick Augustus I – change of religion to protect his ambitions to the Polish crown, although he guaranteed by decree religious freedom for the Protestants and the continuation of the chartered privileges they had enjoyed since 1555 and 1648. The political increase in power, the growing re-conversion to Catholicism in the environment of the Court and the simultaneous loss of Saxony's importance as the hitherto leading country in the union of the Protestant Estates of the Empire, made the guardians of the Lutheran confession in the High Consistory of the Church feel insecure. This development was a challenge to the Church and the Town Council to emphasize Protestant positions. The urgent necessity to replace the old Frauenkirche, which had become dilapidated and too small, by a new building was also supported by the need to represent the rising middle classes and their religious conviction more suitably than before. A copy of the Augsburg Confession with a precious binding was embedded beside the Bible in the foundation of the ambitious building project in 1726 to document the spiritual basis of all activities even those relating to the sovereign. In his memorable sermons at the laying of the foundation stone superintendent Valentin Ernst Löscher expressed his expectation of a stronger renewal of Protestant preaching and life style with the growing building (Fig. 68/69). Already in 1734 he successfully urged the use of the as yet unfinished church for the preaching of sermons, confession and Christian instruction, although this seriously interfered with the ongoing building work in the interior. By this early opening it was intended to create a fait accompli before the church politics of the Saxon-Polish court possibly changed under Augustus the Strong's successor to the throne, Frederick Augustus II, and make clear that Protestantism was the prevailing religion among the citizens of Dresden, that an independent Protestant community life existed and that the society – organized in Diets – and the Town Council were all represented by the building. At the same time they

Fig. 69: Portrait of Valentin Ernst Löscher (1672–1749), Superintendent and High Councillor of the Consistory, copperplate engraving by Christian Fritzsch, 1734

wanted to enrich the townscape of the residential town with this grand domed building.

The structure and the use of the church clearly reflect the religious understanding, the system of values and the hierarchy of the community at that time. With the transfer of old tombs from the Frauenkirche cemetery and the reburials in the crypt floor the need is demonstrated to have the dead near to the living, just as the family vaults situated directly under the private prayer boxes prove (Fig. 43). The area around the altar is accessible to all Christians for receiving the Holy Sacrament while the seats are distributed according to status and property. The sale of more than 2500 of the nearly 3400 seats in the chairs for women on the ground floor, the seats for men on three galleries and of the prayer boxes for noble families was organized on purely commercial grounds as well as the selling of burial chambers in the basement to cover the steeply rising building costs (Fig. 70). It was decided that the balustrades of the boxes should not be marked as private property with coats of arms or other decorations,

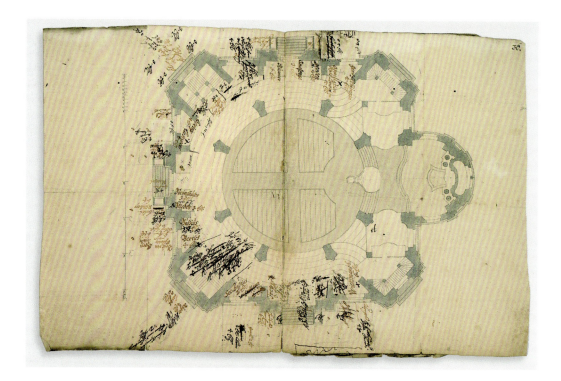

Fig. 70: Ground plan of the ground floor of the Frauenkirche in which the sold seats in the "Betstübchen" and the chairs for women are indicated.
The names of the owners and the width of the prayer boxes are given in ells. The glass private prayer box of Count Wackerbarth is situated above the main entrance of the church. One private prayer box on the ground floor near pier D had been bought by the family of Mayor Behrisch.

i.e. outward equality of the entire Christian community should be expressed but the prices and thereby the seating of the members of the community were clearly differentiated according to one's purse. Disputes lasted for years over the assignment of seats according to one's social position and preferred or rejected juxtaposition of seats. Especially the people from villages which had been incorporated into the parish felt rightly discriminated against compared with the better classes. These problems of order and discord in the new House of God demanded that the priests settle such unchristian disputes and that the supervisory authorities of the church issue fairer regulations. When the continuation of building activities was in danger of being stopped in 1733 the elector Frederick Augustus II ordered the State Treasury to give to the Town Council the sum of 28 366 talers which had been collected in the state for the Protestant exiles from Salzburg. This dishonest misuse of donations was deplored by Löscher in his consecration speech in 1734, but the resources were nevertheless tacitly used for the building.

The use of the Frauenkirche was regulated by detailed rules for divine service for the three churches in the town while most of the important civic occasions had been assigned to the Kreuzkirche as the parish church (Fig. 71). Fewer regular divine services were held and no baptisms took place in the Frauenkirche in spite of its larger capacity. The emphasis lay on Christian instruction and examination, confession and wedding ceremonies, mainly for couples from the surrounding villages. The choirmaster-organist of the Kreuzkirche took over the organization of church music as an additional task to his regular duties; a small group of the Kreuzchor choir under a Head Chorister was responsible for accompanying the divine service. The Frauenkirche had the excellent Silbermann organ but the organists employed were badly paid and soon went to other, better paid posts. After the destruction of the Kreuzkirche from Prussian fire in 1760 in the Seven Years' War the Frauenkirche became the main parish church of the town for more than 30 years and therefore received the baptismal font

	Kreuzkirche	Frauenkirche
on Sundays and holidays:	2 divine services with communion Catechism preaching	1 divine service with communion Catechism examination Theological teaching
on weekdays:	2 divine services Preaching with communion Preaching with confession and penance admonition	1 divine service Catechism examination
on Saturdays:	Confession (afternoon) (about 4 hours)	Confession (before noon) (about 7 hours) Confession and penance admonition Preaching service

Fig. 71: List of the ministrations in the Kreuzkirche and in the Frauenkirche

rescued from the Kreuzkirche. The Frauenkirche was of great importance as the parish priest's place of activity, a safe retreat for Orthodox-Lutheran theology in averting new tendencies of Pietism and enlightenment. Instruction and catechism were at the centre of the pastoral work but this could not prevent the increasing individualisation of attitudes to religion and the retreat to the private sphere. Fewer visitors came to the divine services and the church generally lost in importance since the town had experienced a great loss of inhabitants after the destruction of the town in 1760.

As a decidedly civic church the Frauenkirche always suffered greatly from changes in society, political changes and historical events like the wars of liberation. In 1813 it was, for instance, used by the French occupying forces as a military depot and heavily damaged but was able to be repaired and ceremonially re-consecrated after the retreat of the Napoleonic troops at the instigation of the Russian general governor Prince Repnin-Wolkonski. Shortly after this Saxon volunteers were blessed for the liberation battle in fervently patriotic services. A huge thanksgiving service was held by citizens and returned soldiers of the Landwehr after the Peace of Paris in 1814. Gradually the Frauenkirche took over the role of a national-religious place for celebrating thanksgiving for which it seemed clearly predestined by the emotionally exalting shape of the church. This is probably the reason why the jubilee ceremony on 31st October 1817 recalling the Reformation and later on commemoration services on the occasion of the 330th anniversary of Luther's death in 1846 or the 400th anniversary of his birth in 1883 took place in the Frauenkirche with the building magnificently illuminated (Fig. 72). The monument to Luther by Ernst Rietschel was erected in front of the church in 1883 amid great pomp and with a militantly patriotic consecration sermon. By 1848 The House of God was in the midst of the political play of forces around the bourgeois revolution when, after vehement arguments between the patriotic association, Council and church authorities, an impressive memorial service could finally be held for the progressive parliamentarian Robert Blum who had been shot in Vienna. In 1849 Prussian soldiers, summoned to help by the King, were fighting from the interior of the church against rebels who were hiding in the Hotel de Saxe and Hotel Stadt Rom. After this they made the Frauenkirche a prison for several days. The historic events of the Franco-Prussian War 1870/71 and the attitude of the Protestant church are reflected in the patriotically biased sermons of superintendent Ernst Julius Meier in which the call for a moral-religious renewal among "German Christians" after the war was expressed.

Fig. 72: Illumination on the occasion marking The 300th anniversary of the Reformation in Saxony, 1839

Industrialisation at the end of the 19th century led to a rapid growth of the population and the building of completely new town districts having their own communities. The Frauenkirche was separated from the parish of the Kreuzkirche with its own community in 1878 and developed into an authoritative spiritual centre of the regional Saxon church. Although it is the most splendid of the Protestant town churches it serves a relatively poor community, as it had during the times of the small fishermen's suburb; it has had to battle with the increasing estrangement of the common people from a church mainly influenced by the middle classes. The intensification of the social differences and the resultant political tensions are clearly to be seen. This development came to the notice of the church only after 1930 during the term of office of superintendent Hugo Hahn (Fig. 74). He says in his sermon on the re-consecration of the Frauenkirche in 1932 after the successfully completed restoration of the building: "We are seeing our Gods become visible as idols: the highest possible increase in capital and the production of goods is accompanied by the most dreadful impoverishment and reduction to misery; the most successful development of technology of all times is accompanied by the most desperate helplessness which has ever existed; the most wonderful rise in science is accompanied by an undoubted spiritual impoverishment". Strong stimuli for the spiritual activation of Dresden's Christian inhabitants went out from the services and Bible classes held by this charismatic clergyman and the vesper

services with church music in the Frauenkirche. Religiously motivated resistance with the active participation of professing Christians from the entire region formed here under the pressure from the development of National Socialism in Germany. The Frauenkirche became the centre of the church's struggle against the dictatorship of the brown shirts, the subservient imperial church of the "German Christians" which in 1933 appointed its own Saxon bishop (under the slogan "With Luther and Hitler to faith and national tradition"), declared the church a "cathedral" (Fig. 73) and finally demanded Hahn's dismissal despite the brave resistance of renowned Christian personalities. The superintendent was re-installed in office as a result of tactical changes in the church policy of the Nazi state; he energetically pursued the coming together of the Protestant-Lutheran church in Germany as a basis for church resistance but in 1938 he was finally removed from office and ordered to leave Saxony as head of the "Professing Church". Church life in the Frauenkirche now lay in the hands of the German Christians until its destruction. The cultural-political high regard for the building by the Nazi state allowed the building to be made basically safe and the complete restoration of the Frauenkirche which was in danger of collapse after it had been closed by the building inspection authorities in 1938. The building, apparently stabilised for a long time to come, had only three years left until its tragic ruin in the fire storm of 1945.

The picture of the ruin rising above the rubble has burned itself forever into the minds of numerous witnesses and above all of Dresden artists.

Wilhelm Rudolph (1889–1982), driven by horror, wandered restlessly through the landscape of ruins and recorded the brutal path of destruction in drawings and then in an unforgettable sequence of wood engravings and panel paintings (Fig. 75/92). Johannes Kühl, Edmund Kesting, Bernhardt Kretzschmar, Theodor Rosenhauer or Hans Mroczinski underwent similar experiences after the event which haunted them for years afterwards and drove them to produce effective pictorial statements. Painters of the following generation who were spared going through the Dresden Inferno were conscious of the fractured

Fig. 73: The Frauenkirche as "Cathedral" with swastika flags on the occasion of the appointment of Coch, the Bishop of the "German Christians" on 10th December 1933

Fig. 74: Portrait Hugo Hahn (1886–1957), Superintendent and priest at the Frauenkirche, photograph 1934

Fig. 75: Wilhelm Rudolph (1889–1982)
From the cycle „Dresden destroyed",
1945/46, pen and Indian ink

Fig. 76: Gotthardt Kuehl (1850–1915)
View into the interior of the Frauenkirche,
1910/15, oil on canvas, extract

remains of the church over a long period of time as a gaping wound in the heart of the town and kept the warning memory alive in numerous pictures – be it as paintings, sketches or more in a poster style. Among many others mention should be made of Siegfried Klotz, Christoph Wetzel, Günter Tiedeken, Johannes Heisig, Reinhard Springer or Jürgen Schieferdecker – the pictures speak for themselves and portray the attitude of the artists towards this symbol of a human outrage. Schieferdecker especially interfered with an underlying political motive in this explosive dispute on the character and future of the Frauenkirche memorial, expressing himself in screen prints and collages around 1985.

Throughout all the pictures of the ruin the undamaged original image of the domed building could be seen, crying out for completion. For more than two centuries and over several epochs of different styles the magnificent composition of the town with the domed Frauenkirche had fascinated visual artists in Europe and motivated them to create wonderful works of art. Still today the large vedutas painted by Bernardo Belotto (1721–1780) speak very vividly and accurately of life in the baroque residential town with the Neumarkt and the Frauenkirche in the background (Fig. 53/81). Especially impressive are the paintings by the Romantics, who painted the building within the landscape of the Elbe valley mainly in the idyllic light of morning, the evening or during a moonlit night like Caspar David Friedrich, Carl Gustav Carus (Fig. 78), Johann Christian Dahl or Johann Friedrich Wegener. Pictures with the Frauenkirche could fill a single gallery which would also have to include numerous works of artists from the 20th century like Gotthard Kühl (Fig. 76) and Fritz Beckert (Fig. 77) as late impressionists, Otto Westphal, the expressionists Ernst Ludwig Kirchner or Franz Heckendorf, Edmund Kesting, Ernst Hassebrauk and also good quality photographic art. Something of the unique harmony of landscape, river, town and church emanates from Dresden's "genius loci" and from the radiating power of the "Frauenkirche myth" grown over two centuries and expressed by different artistic hands.

Fig. 77: Fritz Beckert (1877–1962)
Dresden towers, 1940, oil on canvas

Fig. 78: Carl Gustav Carus (1789–1869)
Boat trip on the Elbe, 1827, oil on canvas

The high importance of the Frauenkirche to the history of Dresden church music is above all based on the unusually strong emotional effect and the special acoustics of Bähr's domed building as well as on the outstanding sound quality of Silbermann's organ. Johann Sebastian Bach praised the recently consecrated instrument when he demonstrated his playing ability on 1st December 1736 and two of his talented pupils became the first organists in the Frauenkirche – Christian Heinrich Gräbner (1733–1742) and Gottfried August Homilius (1742–1755) (Fig. 79). A small choir from the Kreuzschule participated with cantatas and motets in the musical performance of the divine services and hence the choirmaster-organists from the Kreuzkirche influenced church music life in the Frauenkirche. Numerous choirmasters and organists achieved high recognition as composers and music teachers. There was, for instance, the Kreuzkirche organist Theodor Christlieb Reinhold who, with his own festive cantatas, contributed to the ceremonial splendour during the laying of the foundation stone in 1726 and the consecration of the Frauenkirche in 1734. During the consecration of the organ in 1736 the audience listened to "outstanding vocal and instrumental music for three choirs..." written by Reinhold and the often admired effect of multi-choir music – even from the upper space under the cupola – was heard. More than 200 church cantatas, 65 motets, oratorios, Passion music and other works have been handed down written by Homilius, who had followed Reinhold as organist of the Kreuzkirche but who worked mainly in the Frauenkirche. In the 19th century civic choral societies made more and more use of the impressive gallery building with its fine acoustics for the performance of great spiritual concerts and oratorios. Richard Wagner composed for the inaugural concert of the General Male Voice Choral Festival in 1843 "The Agape of the Apostles – a biblical scene" exploiting all acoustic possibilities of the unique space of the structure. A great music festival with lavish orchestra and singers was organized in the Frauenkirche in 1850 and the oratorio "David" composed by the musical director of the court orchestra was performed in 1852 as a concert of homage to the King Frederick Augustus II. Once again the church music reflected the constantly changing spirit of the time in the 20th century. The organist Erich Schneider – with the Frauenkirche's own choir founded in 1925 – and the outstanding organist Hans Ander-Donath took care that church music of the highest artistic calibre was continuously cultivated. This was especially important in the times of strife between Church and State after 1933 when spiritual music became a source of strength and consolation for the badly troubled community (Fig. 80).

Fig. 79: Gottfried August Homilius (1714–1785), Organist of the Frauenkirche after 1742, also choirmaster-organist of the Kreuzkirche after 1755

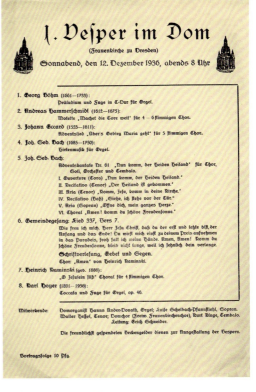

Fig. 80: Programme of the Advent Vesper Service 1936

Constructional repairs, alterations and restoration over a period of 200 years

The great architectural achievement of George Bähr and his fellow-workers in building the Frauenkirche – with the imposing space composition in the interior and the abundant elaborate sculptural forms on the exterior – remains undiminished in spite of the existing constructional weaknesses which, from the very beginning, were inherent in this extraordinary building.

Bähr had developed his building idea consistently as he progressed during the long and contradictory process already described of finding the right shape and in realizing it he went to the limits of what was possible. The construction principles for building the central high rising domed building which he explained to his patrons and the experts who were called in several times in the course of the disputes about the design of the outer cupola in principle proved to be right, from today's engineering point of view, during the planning of the rebuilding. Bähr's idea was based on the assumption that the load exerted by both cupolas would be distributed by the eight internal pillars and the exterior system of load-carrying walls. However, the planned proportionate load distribution to the exterior via the flying buttresses of the curved cupola base and the bracing wing walls between the columns and the area of the outer wall down into the basic stonework was not completely achieved. Settlements in the foundations of the column occurred very early and there existed weak points in the stones and in the material of the column joints which led to compression under high load. The first cracks in the curved base of the cupola, the transverse arches between the columns and in the radial "spieramen" – as George Bähr called the wing walls – had already appeared during construction. These cracks reduced the structural interaction of the load-bearing elements and led to additional weight on the columns and horizontal thrust towards the exterior in the area of the main cornice. This resulted in tilting and subsequent breaking away of parts in the capitals of the pillars as well as crack-formation in the column shafts which already, in 1735, required repairs by means of iron clamps and plaster.

Observation of this damage made the decision on the design of the outer cupola and the lantern so difficult. Each load increase gave rise to the fear that new weaknesses in the already erected substructure would appear. The recommendation made by the director Jean de Bodt to use iron ring anchors in the stonework of the cupola was therefore a decisive contribution to guaranteeing constructional stability. Equally effective were the recommendations made by David Schatz in 1738 for the basic elimination of the damage which had occurred, better load distribution in the bell cages and the thorough covering of cornices and chamfers with sheet metal.

The elimination of damage being caused by stones and material in the joints which were too soft and the use of too hard spandrel stones consisting of "Pläner", a sedimentary rock from the Dresden surroundings, became necessary even during the completion of the exterior building. The very different quality of the sandstone was the reason for early replacements of such delicate constructional elements like window bars in the exterior building as early as 1736. The rough aesthetic effect of the varying stone material gave rise to the wish for a unifying exterior painting which at the same time would provide a certain weather protection for the stonework but only the stonework of the lantern on the cupola received an ochre chalk paint in 1744 (Fig. 81).

Already by 1744 damp in the building caused fungus infestation in the wooden substructure of the so-called "Weiberstühle", chairs on the ground floor which were personally reserved for the well-to-do female citizens. Such damage occurred later in other places like the gallery floors and benches, in the "Betstübchen" (private prayer boxes) or on the floor cover of the spiral ramp in the cupola. It was eliminated by varying methods but could hardly be prevented in an unheated building of that type and with the wood technology then existing.

Fig. 81: The Neumarkt seen from Moritzstraße (extract with first repair work on the curved base of the cupola with rust marks in the areas of the ring anchors), painting by Bernardo Belotto, 1750

The shelling of the Dresden Altstadt by Prussian artillery in the Seven Years War in 1760 was the first serious danger to the Frauenkirche because the imposing domed building represented a favourite target. The shape and solid construction of the building prevented it from being damaged in the attack. Shell holes, cracks from vibration and broken window panes could have only makeshift repairs during this time of war. The court master builder Friedrich August Krubsacius inspected the building in 1765 and found substantial damage in the joints with moisture in the main cornice which were not only the result of military action. Krubsacius stated that a settling of the cupola was causing an additional horizontal thrust on the area of the cornice from the problems with the pillars already described and thus would force the stones out of alignment. The securing of the crack-endangered column shafts by means of clamps or bands was continued in accordance with his recommendations (Fig. 82).

More armed conflicts had adverse consequences especially for the interior furnishings of the church. The Frauenkirche was used as a depot and quarters for the troops during the French occupation in 1813; the pews of the nave were dismantled and stored in the crypt. Because of this all the fittings were badly affected. Damage to furnishings and doors was repaired during the following years, the temporary timber ceiling above the ring opening in the inner cupola was re-opened and the interior of the church was re-painted. Even the wooden arcaded gallery around the inner cupola opening was installed, which had existed in the old design but had not been fitted for reasons of cost.

The first extensive repair to the exterior of the building became necessary in 1820/21 after a survey of damage caused by moisture penetration and the crumbling of stones. The movements in the building already mentioned led to the cracking of joints in the curved base of the cupola and the cornice areas. Rainwater came in, plants rooted and destroyed the mortar in the joints which during frosty periods were forced open more and more, so that pieces of stones fell off. The repair work was limited to the clearing of plants from the stonework, rejointing of the joints and the securing of loose stones. Highly endangered areas of the cornice were covered with copper.

The further worsening of the condition of the building led to a basic refurbishment of the entire House of God. Heavy damage to the bell cases and the substructure of the towers required repair work as early as 1857, but the defects could not be eliminated forever. The dynamic load on the stone building by the vibration of the bells had already been mentioned by David Schatz as reason for the damage but the matter had never been subsequently investigated. Now the building was almost completely surrounded by scaffolding for work on all the stonework (Fig. 83). Damaged spots were repaired with new sandstone, loose stones were secured, damaged window bars and window panes were replaced, brittle mortar in the joints was scratched out and replaced by cement mortar. (This use of Portland cement turned out to be very problematic for the maintenance of sandstone buildings.) The lantern received a new copper cover, the orb and cross were repaired, the main cornice and roof areas were covered anew with copper and for the first time a lightning conductor was installed. Defective plaster and stuccowork in the inner cupola,

Fig. 82: Exposed upper capital area of the northeast pillar with old iron band and clamps, 1932

Fig. 83: Cupola of the Frauenkirche with scaffolding, drawing by Adolph v. Menzel, 1880

gallery balustrades and column capitals were repaired and the installations in the backward-facing prayer boxes on the galleries were removed and replaced by rows of benches; the wooden floors and doors also had to be repaired. This extensive repair work then required the renewal of the paintwork in the church; organ, altar and pulpit with the choir screen were re-gilded and Grone's paintings in the cupola were entirely redone by Ludwig Kriebel. The inner opening of the cupola was closed again, this time by a flat glass pyramid and new draught-excluding doors were installed in the four staircase towers to reduce undesirable draughts in the church. Air heating with four furnaces in the main basement and smoke outlets at the side of the choir was installed in 1871 but it did not prove successful because of the pollution caused in the interior of the church (Fig. 84).

Repairs on the exterior building became necessary again in 1887/92, especially on the cupola, the roof of the chancel and the tops of the towers. This time an attempt was made to eliminate the well-known problems of stone weathering

and mortar erosion and consequent damp, by using black-coloured cement mortar for stone replacements and filling the joints. This had to be redone in 1908.

Crushed stones on the capitals had to be replaced repeatedly and vaulting had to be repaired. A connection to the city's long-distance heating system was made in 1907 and radiators were installed; the church was supplied with electric lighting; paintwork and gilding were renewed and pews, altar and organ were recoloured.

Experts repeatedly drew attention to damage caused by movements in the building between 1912 and 1921 together with damage caused by water entering and the fall of structural parts all of which urgently required remedial measures. Basic repairs were possible between 1924 and 1932 under the supervision of the municipal building director Paul Wolf (Fig. 85). It was again intended to strengthen the internal structure of the columns carrying the cupola, replace destroyed stones and secure overloaded areas of the columns by means of steel bands (Fig. 86/87). It was decided to replace affected timber by steel girders because of the extensive damage in the galleries (Fig. 88). Destroyed stones and gaping joints were repaired with sandstone to enable safe water drainage. The extreme case was that broken corner pieces of the main cornice measuring 3.2 × 1.2 × 0.6 m had to be replaced (Fig. 89). A new type of bituminous material was used for sealing especially endangered joints in the curved

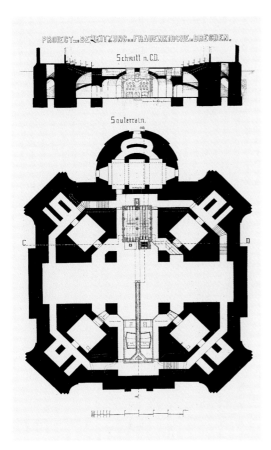

Fig. 84: Project for a heating plant – cross and longitudinal section through the basement floor, drawing by E. Kelling, 1868

Fig. 85: South side of the Frauenkirche with scaffolding, Photograph, around 1921

base of the cupola (Fig. 90). It was a surprise to find that re-used slabs from tombs of the old Frauenkirche cemetery, consisting of soft stone used for sculptures, had been used for the heavily weathered wall slabs at the base of the building which had now to be replaced.

In spite of all the thoroughness with which the repair work was carried out – limited also because of the restricted financial means of the Protestant Consistory – further decay showed that the building work could not cease. It was disturbing to observe new settlements, cracks in the vault and the penetration of moisture. The architect Arno Kiesling was ordered to make a rigorous survey of the church and the recognized specialist for spatial structures at the Technische Hochschule, Professor Georg Rüth, was commissioned in 1938 to give an expert assessment of structural damage to the building. Rüth's investigations, his scientific conclusions and the renovation measures started and supervised by him are exemplary even in the opinion of today's experts. He saw that the settlements of the column foundations were a decisive reason for the load shifts and deformations in the upper zones of the building. He joined together the individual foundations by a strong ring of reinforced concrete arches, exerting pressure down against the ground, which still today bear the loads in the rebuilt church.

Fig. 86: Southwest pillar of the cupola during the replacement of crushed stones, 1931

Fig. 87: Remains of an interior pillar girded with steel in 1930, recovered during rubble clearing in 1997

They are tightly inserted by hydraulic force between the eight foundations. The second long term measure was that Rüth had three reinforced concrete anchors installed on the inner side of the outer cupola shell which were connected to the stonework of the cupola (Figs. 91). They could better keep the vault in shape and guarantee stability than the forged iron anchors installed by George Bähr under the exterior surface layer of the cupola, which had slackened under the great peripheral tensile stress. This repair work carried out under Rüth was the first securing-work on the Frauenkirche building to investigate the fundamental reasons for the damage and could be regarded as providing a long-lasting remedy. After that a general restoration of the interior was carried out under Rüth but only two years later all these efforts for the preservation of this magnificent building were ruined during a single night of bombing.

Fig. 88: Repairs on the galleries, installation of steel girders, 1931

Fig. 89: Replacement of a large base stone

Fig. 90: Repair work on the cupola, around 1930

Fig. 91: Reinforced concrete ring anchors of the Frauenkirche, strengthening cage on the inner side of the exterior shell

Fig. 92: Wilhelm Rudolph (1889–1982)
The destroyed Dresden, 1952, oil on canvas

Destruction, treatment of the ruin, efforts towards rebuilding

Dresden's terrible destruction in the bombing on 13th and 14th February 1945 reached its tragic end with the collapse of the burnt out Frauenkirche on the morning of February 15th. There is hardly a more impressive description of what had happened than the written report by Hermann Weinert, Senior Church Inspector, who witnessed the last hours of the church: "The flame vase of the bell tower above door C collapsed as a result of the bombs falling on Neumarkt ... The devastating force of burning houses around was growing from hour to hour so that about two o'clock in the morning red-hot lava poured into the interior of the church through the heat-shattered church windows between doors G and F, which had not yet been walled up. The galleries and the "Betstübchen" (private prayer boxes) were immediately set on fire and finally the pews were seized by the flames... At about five o'clock the undersigned, by summoning up his remaining energy, succeeded in rescuing refugees who were suffering from the thick smoke developing in the church cellars. They were made to form a chain leading between the blazing Cosel Palace and the Academy of Arts to the Brühl Terrace... On Thursday, February 15th, around eleven o'clock I was walking into the dead city looking for the cupola of the church. To my great shock I looked into the void in the milky fog. An hour before my wife had witnessed the tragedy when she was searching for me. After an initial crackle the cupola slowly collapsed and then the outer walls of the church burst with an enormous bang and a pitch-black cloud of dust filled the surrounding area."

Professor Georg Rüth had already died from heart failure in the night of the bombing at the sight of the burning town. The walling up of all window holes ordered by him and the evacuation of the just recently renewed pews of the church, recommended by the curator of monuments Walter Bachmann, had unfortunately

Fig. 93: Dresden, the inner Altstadt, view from the west to the ruins around the Frauenkirche, 1945

Fig. 94:
System worked by Arno Kiesling for the archaeological rubble clearing, 5th November 1948

INVENTARISIERUNG

der vorhandenen Steine der Frauenkirche, die infolge Kriegseinwirkung am 14.Februar 1945 in Brand geraten war und am 15.Februar 1945 vormittags gegen 11 Uhr einstürzte.

Erklärung der Bezeichnungen und Nummern der Steine.

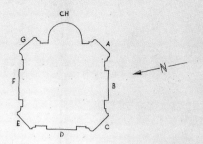

Die Ecktürme und Seiten der Frauenkirche werden nach den alten Eingangstüren, die große römische Buchstaben im Schlußstein trugen, bezeichnet.

A	Süd-Ost Eckturm
B	Südseite
C	Süd-West Eckturm
D	Westseite
E	Nord-West Eckturm
F	Nordseite
G	Nord-Ost Eckturm
H	Westseite
CH	Choranbau Westseite
K	Kuppel
LH	Laternenhals
L	Laterne

Die Formsteine werden noch mit kleinen römischen Buchstaben bezeichnet.

s	Sockel
g	Gurtgesims
hs	Hauptgesims einschl. Architrav und Attika
ts	Tambourgesims

Steine unbekannter Herkunft werden mit X bezeichnet.

Jeder Stein bekommt außerdem eine laufende Nummer, die zunächst rein zeitlich nach dem Anfall festgelegt wird.
Beispiel: Hauptgesimsstück am G-Turm G hs 5
(Nummer 5 besagt, daß bereits von dem Hauptgesims 5 Steine vorhanden sind.)

Die glatten Steine werden nur mit dem römischen Buchstaben und einer Nummer versehen.
Beispiel: G 23, A 22, usw.

Alle Steine der Innenräume werden genau wie die Außensteine bezeichnet und bekommen dazu ein großes römisches I.
Die Innenpfeiler in der selben Reihenfolge wie die Außenbezeichnung.
Die genaue Lage der Steine wird in den Ansichtszeichnungen eingetragen.

5.November 1948   gez. A. Kiesling

Making an Inventory of the existing stones of the Frauenkirche, which – as a result of warfare – caught fire on 14th February and collapsed in the morning of 15th February around 11 o'clock.

Explanation of the indicated letters and numbers of the stones.

The corner towers and sides of the Frauenkirche are named after the old entrance doors having large Roman letters on the key stone.

A	southeast corner tower
B	south side
C	southwest corner tower
D	west side
E	northwest corner tower
F	north side
G	northeast corner tower
H	west side
CH	chancel west side
K	cupola
LN	lantern neck
L	lantern

Shaped stones are marked with small Roman letters.

a	base
g	belt course
hs	main cornice including architrave and attic
ts	tambour cornice

Stones of unknown origin are marked with X.

Each stone gets in addition to this a consecutive number, which is given purely on the basis of the time of recovery.

Example: Piece of main cornice at G-tower G hs 5 (number 5 means that already 5 stones of the main cornice have been found).

Smooth stones are given only Roman letters and a number.
Example: G 23, A 22, etc.

All stones of interior rooms are marked in the same way as stones of the exterior and get an additional large Roman I.
The interior pillars are marked in the same sequence as the exterior parts. The exact position of the stones is entered in the profile drawings.

5th November 1948
sgd. A. Kiesling

been only partially carried out. These protective measures might have prevented the disaster based on the fact that the domed building basically secured by Rüth had miraculously withstood the bombing. Luckily nobody among those seeking shelter had died in the cellars, but the community of the Frauenkirche had practically been wiped out with the destruction of this House of God and the built-up area of the city centre (Fig. 92/93).

First of all everything which could be rescued was recovered out of the accessible basement areas in March 1945 including evacuated works of art from the Sophienkirche, church equipment and archival documents on the Frauenkirche and fortunately the complete building documents on the repair work between 1937–1942. The architect Arno Kiesling and Professor Rüth's colleague Dr. Walter Henn went on a preliminary inspection tour and made an inventory of the ruin and – as the best experts in the matter – were ordered to assess the stability of the ruins and prepare the necessary safety measures for the heap of rubble. The participating experts, the Conservation Department of Saxony and the Church of Saxony were convinced that the ruin should be preserved for later rebuilding and protected against destructive acts.

It was not until 1948 that the careful clearing of the rubble and the recovering of precious ashlars could be started with money from the "rebuilding lottery". Kiesling and Henn were again entrusted with the planning and instructions for the work and immediately developed a special, sophisticated system for taking an inventory of the recovered pieces of rubble, distinguishing between stones from the entrance axes A to G, the horizontal areas of the building, exterior and interior building and stones for giving shape or for mere infill (Fig. 94). This system became the basis for "archaeological rubble clearing" when start-

ing the rebuilding work 45 years later. It was in the winter of 1948/49 that about 600 m³ of reusable stones were recovered, measured, registered and brought by means of a temporary railway to the Salzgasse where they were piled up in an orderly fashion (Fig. 95). The work was then stopped because of a shortage of money – despite urgent appeals by the Conservation Authorities which continued to protect the ruin as best as they could. In 1952 the altar wall, which fortunately had been protected by the organ gallery from total destruction, (Fig. 96), was secured against weathering and vandalism by walling up the whole area. With wise foresight for future development – which, even then, envisaged the later "archaeological reconstruction" – the Conservation Department of Saxony under Dr. Hans Nadler entrusted the architect Arno Kiesling – who had already surveyed the building during the general repair of the church between 1937–1942 – with the total documentation of the church by making drawings on the basis of rescued documents. The coloured representations were the work of the painter Willy Trede who had once worked as restorer in the Frauenkirche. This work was carried out between 1949 and 1959 and finally became an important source for the rebuilding planning after 1990 (Fig. 97).

The entire area with the ruins in Dresden's inner city had been declared a reconstruction area after 1950 and was now under the control of the State. During the large-scale rubble clearance (Fig. 98) repeated attempts were made to take away even the few remaining pieces of the Frauenkirche. It was thanks to the Conservation Department that the original stones in the heap of rubble, which in the meantime had become covered in vegetation, remained untouched. The area of the ruins was massively endangered in 1959 when the city administration ordered that the stored stones should be taken from the Salz-

Fig. 95: Dresden, Frauenkirche. Two sunflowers from the cornice and capital remains by J. Chr. Feige, recovered and registered rubble stones in the Salzgasse, photograph, 1948

Fig. 96: Dresden, Frauenkirche. Front view of altar fragment after two years without the protective walling up, photograph 1947

gasse to the Elbe river bank to provide enough parking space for the state ceremony on the occasion of the re-opening of the art collection. After massive protests from the curators of monuments, it was possible to have half of the precious ashlars returned. Finally, in 1963 an agreement was reached that the ruin would be preserved as a memorial, cleared of wild vegetation and surrounded by a protecting hedge of roses symbolizing new life (Fig. 99). A plaque commemorating the builder and the destruction of the church was installed on a remaining wall of staircase tower E in 1967. A group of volunteers in the cultural society of the GDR took care of the ruin while the Church in Saxony as owner of the building was not in a position to do so and perhaps wanted to disassociate itself from the use of the ruin for political purposes. An annually growing number of people – particularly young people of the Christian Peace Movement – gathered, especially after 13th February 1982, in front of the ruin with candles in quiet memory of the victims of the destruction and in protest against the global armament race (Fig. 2/3). After that the Town Council prepared the area around the Frauenkirche for demonstrations organised by the State on the memorial day and documented the official political attitude with a bronze memorial plaque installed in the ground on which the "living" were reminded "to fight against imperialist barbarism, for peace and the happiness of the people".

Over a long period after the war the position of the Protestant Church of Saxony concerning the building heritage of the Frauenkirche was cautious and unclear, although the will for rebuilding had initially predominated. This was understandable in view of the heavy destruction and the general dilapidation of church buildings, the repressive church politics of the GDR government and the particular situation of the community in the inner city of Dresden. There was no need for the extraordinary expenditure involved in the rebuilding of such a big parish church and so it could not be justified. Church resources had been exhausted by the first rubble clearance and the protective walling up of the altar. There was a proposal in 1948 to found an "Association of Friends of the Frauenkirche", however it was not done because of political considerations. In 1953 the Protestant Synod of Saxony seriously discussed the rebuilding of the Frauenkirche but could not decide on this step during the difficult situation of the church at that time. The Conservation Department as the main authority for the preservation of the still extant original material

Fig. 98: Dresden, view into the destroyed Münzgasse during rubble clearing, photograph 1952

Fig. 99: Dresden, Frauenkirche. The collapsed west gable – 35 years after destruction under blooming roses, photograph, 1980

Fig. 97: Arno Kiesling and Willy Trede Frauenkirche, north-south cross section, sheet with final colouring 232/125 cm

Fig. 100: Dresden, Frauenkirche. Making the ruin safe at the southwest staircase tower

acted with great skill -especially in the person of professor Dr. Hans Nadler – and kept the rebuilding of the church in view over several decades. There were always responsible personalities in politics and administration who supported this plan in spite of all kinds of personal abuse. The doyen among Dresden's art historians Dr. Fritz Löffler publicized the case for the rebuilding of the church with great stubbornness and visionary persuasive power until the end of his life in 1988. Even in 1982 suggestions by the newly appointed chief curator at the Institute for the Conservation of Monuments Dr. Gerhard Glaser to use the cellar under the choir of the ruin for services or exhibitions were not taken up by the church authorities. Only the new development in public perception of the Frauenkirche ruin as a memorial for peace and reconciliation as well as various suggestions concerning town planning for the city centre of Dresden gradually changed the attitude of the Saxon Church towards their House of God which was so rich in history. It was mainly superintendent Christoph Ziemer who understood the signs of the time and supported the idea that the church should take over its rights and obligations. In 1985 it was decided to clear the heap of rubble professionally, to make the ruins secure and create a sacred space open to the sky which at that time and at this place seemed to correspond most closely with the self-image of the Protestant Christians . The curators of monuments however insisted that the stones should remain in the heap of rubble until rebuilding was possible. Only in October 1989 did the city of Dresden entrust Dr. Roland Zepnik with the planning of measures to guarantee the safety of the ruin with respect to the requirements of future rebuilding (Fig. 100).

Four months later the "Call from Dresden" – expressed on 13th February 1990 – inspired a development gaining an ever spreading basis which could finally lead only to the completion of the new Frauenkirche. The responsible people in the Saxon Church together with the building specialists of all Protestant churches in Germany in a memorandum distanced themselves from the efforts for rebuilding and pleaded for the preservation of the memorial of the ruin as a symbol even in January 1991. At the same time a technical meeting was held by a group of supporters of rebuilding to discuss the basis for the most authentic reconstruction of the building in accordance with archaeological principles. The differences of opinion on the legitimacy of such reconstructions of monuments went right across the world of experts and many Christians uttered objections against such an expensive project in view of the manifold misery in the world. It was Bishop Dr. Johannes Hempel who, together with the art historian Dr. Joachim Menzhausen, was

Fig. 101: Hanns Hopp, Planning Dresden's rebuilding (extract), June 1945

Fig. 102: Kurt W. Leucht, Investigation of the inner city – area of cultural and central function (extract), Town Planning Office, 10th February 1948

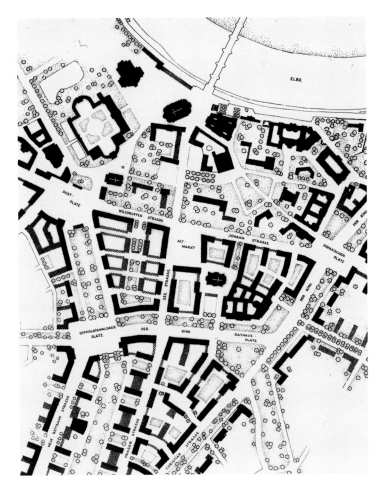

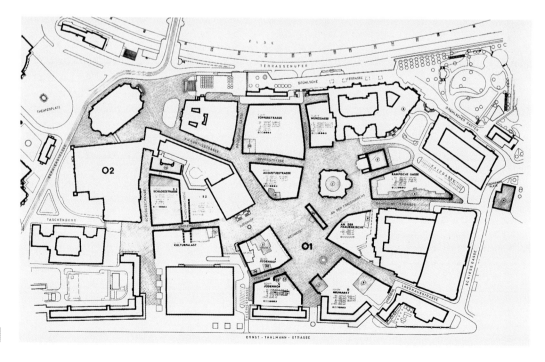

able to convince the majority of the Synod in Saxony to approve the rebuilding of the Frauenkirche in February 1991 with the words: "It is better to heal a wound than to leave it open...".

The will to rebuild the church as an outstanding example of baroque church building and embodiment of the Protestant understanding of the divine service which had inspired many Christians and art connoisseurs since its destruction had always been accompanied by the hope of restoring the compactness of Dresden's townscape by its rebuilding. Already in one of the first meetings on the "Grand Plan for the Rebuilding of Dresden" in 1945 the municipal building officer Dr. Herbert Conert called the Frauenkirche a highlight in the town silhouette which would be both needed and desired in the future. The ruin of the Frauenkirche was in the following years regarded as a fixed point in most of the rebuilding plans for the city centre and its space was kept free from new buildings in spite of all the rigorous town-planning suggestions for the future structure of the built-up area (Fig. 101).

Suggestions were also brought forward in 1948, expressing the new spirit of socialist town planning, for a "Pavilion of Visual Arts" or a dancing school exactly on this site (Fig. 102). Later plans brought forward by the Dresden Town Council, students and professors of the Dresden University of Technology or competition plans of various groups of architects made clear that the Frauenkirche was always shown as "a ruin to be rebuilt" and it was carefully embedded in the rebuilt Neumarkt area or surrounded by a park (Fig. 103). The height of the cornice of the Frauenkirche had always determined the height of the buildings in the city centre (Fig. 104). But with the planning of a "High-rise building for Socialist Culture" on the Altmarkt it was intended deliberately to ignore this rule.

Thanks to the persistent resistance of Dresden architects this was prevented by proposing better plans for today's "Palace of Culture". They ensured that the municipal plans for the area of the Frauenkirche included more and more of the old structural development on Neumarkt.

A small planning office had given an impetus in 1967–1976 with the rebuilding of the two wings of the old Cosel Palace and made the location their office right by the ruin of the Frauenkirche. On the basis of the results of an international design seminar the city administration finally laid down in "Town-planning instructions" (Fig. 105) the historic ground plan of the town in the Neumarkt area including the Frauenkirche. In 1988 the architects Dieter Schölzel and Dr. Walter Köckeritz made a proposal for an impressive memorial in the interior of the cleared ruin, now permanently made safe, At the same time they suggested to Bishop Dr. Hempel to go beyond these plans and envisage the complete rebuilding. They were part of a team of architects and town planners set up to work out design principles for a future building development on the Neumarkt with historically faithful reconstructed buildings and new contemporary buildings. Such commitment finally bore fruit with the rebuilding and consecration of the new Frauenkirche in October 2005. The surroundings of the church are also being laid out gradually and will give the dominating building its town-planning frame, although many hopes for the preservation of the historic traces below ground, for authentically restored facades or even for partial retention of the structure of old court houses will not be realized.

Fig. 103: Model of the building design, Department for town planning and architecture of the Dresden Town Council, 1965

Fig. 104: Comparison of options for the cultural-historic centre by Gunter Just and Horst Witter, 1977

Fig. 105: "Town planning rules" for housing construction, layout of the city centre, office of Dresden's main architect, 1983

Early history and planning preparation for the rebuilding

Encouraged by the feverish atmosphere of political changes and the break-up of the GDR in the autumn of 1989 a small group of Dresden citizens expressed their vision for the rebuilding of the Frauenkirche as a joint future task in the "Call from Dresden", cleverly taking advantage of the opportune moment: Time was ripe for a new consciousness of the obligations of heritage, for making people aware of their civic energies and for having an active influence on the processes of social change. It was still necessary bravely to overcome uncertainty and fear and gain important partners in politics, the church, culture and the media for the huge Frauenkirche task – sometimes in conspiratorial ways. This was successful and the ground was prepared when the "Citizens' initiative for the rebuilding of the Frauenkirche" under the chairmanship of Professor Ludwig Güttler appeared before the press with their appeal (Fig. 107). The seeds of hope for the resurrection of the magnificent domed building, Dresden's old crown, germinated very quickly. The call for help spread like wildfire in Germany and soon across the international public, especially among Dresdeners living far away but still with a special attachment to their home town. Innumerable people, among them famous personalities with great charisma, became members of the Fördergesellschaft für den Wiederaufbau, founded in 1991. Many groups and associations of supporters were founded within a few months. They canvassed for donations with huge optimism and great involvement in the most varied ways and thereby helped to lay the financial foundation for the rebuilding.

The initiators had hardly dared to reckon with such self-dynamism. The commitment of the curators of monuments and town planners over many decades had obviously paid off for they had kept alive the confidence in a later rebuilding of the ruin. Even in 1953 Dr. Hans Nadler, the head of the Conservation Department in Saxony, spoke of the possibility of an "anastylosis" of the building (only with the original pieces of rubble) and the curators of monuments, in their pleading for a reconstruction always referred to the extraordinary abundance of precise documents and plans from the time the church was built and the later well documented repairs. Although original plans designed by George Bähr for the new building hardly exist, numerous copper engravings had been created parallel to the building of the church by Christian Philipp Lindemann … They show the exterior shape, the inner structure and the furnishing of the church according to the planning stages between 1731 and 1734. Experts, who were called in later, were asked to investigate structural damage and the stability of the stone building and prepared measurements, drawings and crack mapping as the basis for their assessment. The master builder Johannes Theodor Zumpe (1863/64) produced exact sections through the building and the first plans for repairing the lantern. The municipal building officer Paul Wolf and the senior master builder Karl Pinkert prepared precise drawings of the church and the specific damaged zones during the extensive

Fig. 107:
Press conference of the "Citizen's initiative" in the Dresden Bellevue Hotel in Große Meißner Straße on 12th February 1990

From left to right sitting: Prof. Dr. Heinrich Magirius, Prof. Dr.-Ing. Hans Nadler (half-hidden), Dr. Karlheinz Blaschke, Prof. Ludwig Güttler, Dr.h.c. Folkert Ihmels, Dr.-Ing. Otto Baer, standing: Dr.-Ing. Walter Köckeritz, Dipl.-Ing. Dieter Schölzel, Dr.-Ing. Roland Zepnik, Dr. rer. nat. Rudolph Stephan, Dipl.-Ing. Steffen Gebhardt, Dipl.-Jur. Dieter Zuber, Prof. Dr.-Ing. Hermann Rühle, Dr.-Ing. Hans-Joachim Jäger, three representatives of the press, Dr. Hans-Joachim Neidhardt

Fig. 106: The Frauenkirche ruin before rebuilding, 1992

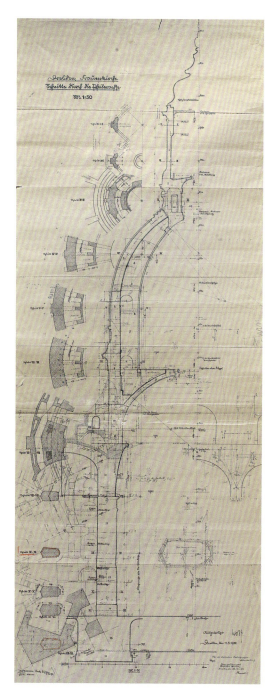

Fig. 108: Frauenkirche, vertical section through the cupola (extract), drawing by Wolf/Häfler, 1932

repair work between 1924 and 1932 (Fig. 108). Additional plans were also prepared during the securing of the building between 1936 and 1943 on the basis of thorough measurements by Arno Kiesling. Georg Rüth let his younger fellow-workers Henn and Siegel enter all cracks in the building into these plans so that he could draw up conclusions and proposals for repair from studying their extent (Fig. 109/110). The developments of the time made it possible for more and more photographs to be taken of repair work, the interior and the exterior building taken from every angle in the town. All these documents had survived miraculously during wartime in their places of safe-keeping and the heap of rubble still concealed invaluable original material which only had to be uncovered. From the first post-war years the plans of Kiesling and Trede still existed. No other building destroyed in Dresden had more extensive and accurate documentation.

It was now possible to justify convincingly the idea of archaeological reconstruction of the important sacred building supported by new contributions from science, monument conservation and society. It became the programme of the Fördergesellschaft für den Wiederaufbau which was then formulated in the "Guidelines" of the Frauenkirche Foundation on 12th February 1995. The building should be completely rebuilt as a church on strict historical lines using George Bähr's plans as a basis with much of the historic fabric of the building and new Saxon sandstone and taking into account the principles of master building and the work of craftsmen, as well as the latest technological knowledge. It was the declared aim to recreate this unique work of baroque architecture as authentically as possible and thereby close a gaping wound in Dresden's famous townscape.

In spite of this, considerable resistance based on scientific, aesthetic and philosophical arguments against the rebuilding of the largely destroyed original was expressed among experts on conservation and art historians. Professional circles pointed to the principle that the ruin, as it was, had to be regarded as a monument to be protected and that the monument would vanish with the rebuilding. This had been laid down in 1964 in the "Venice Charter" as the direction and culture of European conservationism. This agreement was quite justified in view of numerous historicising reproductions of lost architecture.

The Knochenhaueramtshaus in Hildesheim, the Zeil buildings in Frankfurt a. M., the market square in Mainz or the Leibnitz house in Hanover are today regarded as questionable replacements of monuments, to name only a few examples in Germany. Critics raised the reproach that the

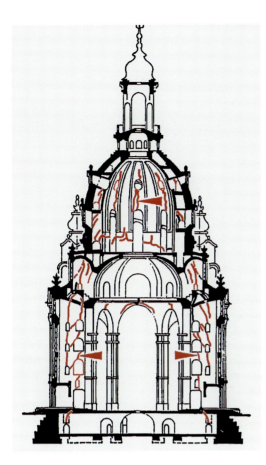

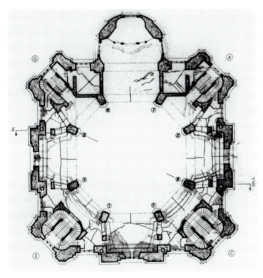

Fig. 109: Frauenkirche, 1937, drawing with cracks, after Georg Rüth, north-south cross section

Fig. 110: Frauenkirche, Georg Rüth (1880–1945), drawing with cracks on the level of the third gallery floor, 1938

rebuilding of the Frauenkirche would result in a mere copy or replica which would neither be a historic monument nor an authentic work of art and actually a correction to history and a retreat from the present, even a capitulation before the task of creating contemporary buildings of equal value. Already in 1991 German conservationists declared in a meeting in Potsdam about the reconstruction plans for the Frauenkirche and the Berlin Palace: "... The erection of reproductions of lost monuments can only be of importance for the work in the present day. Such copies cannot be monuments recalling great achievements of the past in their full sense and keeping alive the memory of historic processes with their heights and depths. Conservationists are responsible only for historical evidence which cannot be reproduced and must warn when there is a threat to the possibility for remembrance in the public arena." For this reason the Deutsche Stiftung Denkmalschutz (German Foundation for the Conservation of Monuments) did not participate in financing the rebuilding from the very beginning.

This dispute led to the inner conviction that the Frauenkirche as a unique building of the past and as a monument of destruction of great symbolic significance required a specific approach. The mere securing and conservation of the ruin, the preservation of the latest condition of the heap of rubble could not be seen to be compatible with the rebuilding plans for the Neumarkt area with its lively urban density. Nobody among those who still had an idea of the inexpressible sufferings of the people in war and destruction could possibly want to have an aesthetically improved memorial ruin. Such a memorial would also be exposed to dilapidation ... No – the advocates of rebuilding together with the curators of monuments in Saxony felt that it was an obligation of our time to rebuild this House of God, which represented a profession of faith in stone by the creators of the building, not just as a decorative copy but as a faithful resurrection of the original. This lies at the heart of the term "archaeological rebuilding" which subsequently had to be defined with clear instructions for all participants. The process had clearly and distinctively to be separated from all proposals to erect a new building in the spirit of our time with its own interpretation and modern technologies because faith had to be kept with the many donors who supported the rebuilding in accordance with the original. The reconstruction of the interior remained for a long time uncertain and disputed because it had to be decided which of the historic aspects of colour and furnishing over the 200 years of existence should be adhered to. The

Fig. 111: Pulsnitz, town church St. Nicolai, view of the interior restored in 1995 with a view to the organ

decision was finally made to attempt the restoration of the baroque colouring by means of the few colours remaining on pieces of rubble, the reminiscence of the painters who had taken part in the restoration before the war and by comparisons with extant church furnishings made by the Frauenkirche masters (Fig. 111).

With clarity now achieved on the theoretical principles of treatment the Dresden Frauenkirche Foundation, as the patron, could formulate the considerations on the use of the future church building. It was above all the intention to use the Frauenkirche again as a living House of God, to reach many people with divine services, church music and other church performances and to have, especially in the lower rooms, a memorial area as a reminder of the victims and the sufferings in the past and a place for concerts, art events, lectures, meetings and symposia.

An underground exterior building should accommodate everything necessary for secondary functions. Last but not least, the church should become a special point of attraction for visitors to the town wanting to experience the interior and enjoy the splendid view over the townscape with the Elbe valley by going up to the lantern on top of the cupola. The spirit and dignity of the sacred building should set the standard for all possible usage as well as for campaigning for the necessary finance to allow rebuilding.

Thus the framework was established in which experienced and reliable partners for scientific and technological preparation as well as for planning of the rebuilding could operate. Professional advice and supervision were the undoubted responsibility of the Conservation Department with its specific knowledge gathered during decades of work, but who could be entrusted with the highly complex planning of the building work, the technical equipment or the surveying work? The following firms were entrusted with the main planning and preparation work:

- Planungsbüro Versammlungsstätten under Dieter Schölzel
  (preliminary investigations for the whole project and approval planning)
- Architekten- und Ingenieurgesellschaft IPRO Dresden under Dr. Bernd Kluge
  (main planning for all architectural and technical work as well as for the coordination of all other professional planning work
- Ingenieurgemeinschaft of Professor Fritz Wenzel/Karlsruhe and Dr. Wolfram Jäger/Radebeul (structural planning and scientific accompaniment during rubble clearing)
- Ingenieurvermessung Dresden
  (surveying work for rubble clearing and construction work)
- Spezialbau SPESA Nordhausen and Sächsische Sandsteinwerke Pirna
  (archaeological rubble clearing)

At the same time the securing work already mentioned for the chancel was carried out to guarantee that this part could be included without danger to the entire building.

It was the task of the team of experts working on this huge project to develop a precise strategy for action on the basis of the main task of archaeological rubble clearing and archaeological rebuilding, to prepare the methodology and the division of labour among the participating firms as well as the first steps of rubble clearing. The rubble clearing in accordance with archaeological principles was above all aimed at the exact reconstruction of the original geometry of the building and at rescuing as many as possible of the re-usable parts, their identification and correct allocation in the new structure. This was supported by the exact documentation of the corresponding places of discovery in the heap of rubble and with this knowledge it was hoped to find the explanation for the process of the collapse and more precise reasons for the failure of Bähr's cupola construction. All information on the building, its materials, colouring, the contemporary working technologies and damage which had occurred in the past contained in the pile of debris was to be collected and registered with scientific accuracy. The subsequent archaeological rebuilding was made possible and could be soundly justified only with this knowledge. It

Fig. 112: The heap of rubble at the beginning of the rubble-clearing with the geodetic network shown in one area, seen from a crane

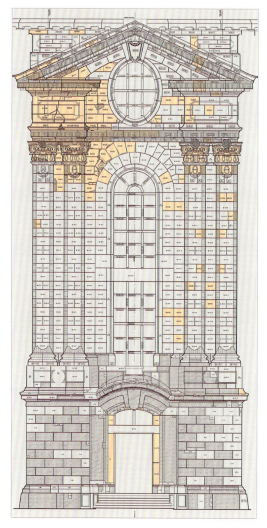

Fig. 113: Comparison of a façade drawing with the implemented partial stone building at the west façade at entrance "D". The intact exterior wall is indicated in grey. Old and new stones are marked in yellow and white respectively and numbered.

was decided to clear away the heap of rubble layer by layer as with a surface excavation. All pieces found were provided with a serial number and the positioning of the pieces was measured and digitally photographed in their fallen position by means of a grid system (Fig. 112). All dimensional and material details, the state of preservation, the probable original position in the building and future usability had to be determined after the careful recovery of the stones – as it had been methodically envisaged by Henn and Kiesling in 1945. The entirety of all data on each piece found had to be stored in a large data system. All information on the registered rubble material could consequently be interconnected and analysed by means of electronic data processing in order to position as many old stones as possible in the right place in the new building. Already during setting up the inventory on the site it was possible to enter by hand the positively assigned parts into the plans of the facade. Complete computer drawings of the facades showing all recovered stones were made on the basis of the last stone structure before the destruction after having brought together all information on the pieces found (Fig. 113). These plans were meant to serve as a later basis for the stone technology in the planning of the rebuilding. The registered high-grade stone material was kept ready for further preparation in a logistically perfectly organized shelf store beside the site. The mere backing stones were stored for later use on the Elbe river bank near the Albertbrücke (Fig. 115/116).

The carefully considered and implemented process of archaeological rubble clearing was the basis for the planning of archaeological rebuilding which required no less effort. This form of reconstruction required the most exact and demonstrable knowledge of the original building including exterior and interior shape, geometry of all internal spaces and structural parts, type, properties and origin of the building mate-

Fig. 114: Working with the 3D computer model, IPRO office

Fig. 115: Shelf store, sawing house and stonemasons' sheds on the Neumarkt

Fig. 116: Stone store on the Elbe meadows upstream of Albert bridge

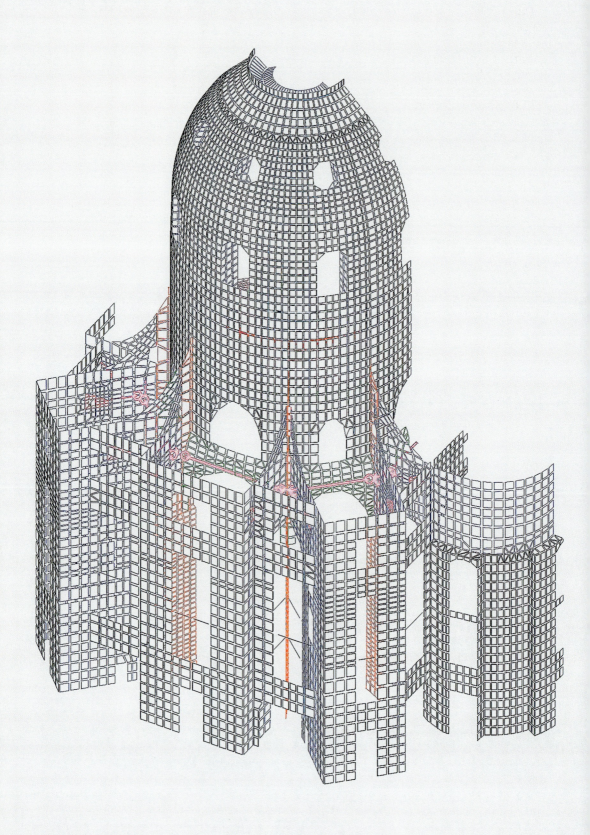

Fig. 117: Network of units of half the structure of the church building for final structural comparative tests, Jörg Peter, Martin Hertenstein, 1993

rials, colouring and type of surface as well as historic building and joining techniques. The drawing up of an inventory of what existed before the construction with the exact geometrical dimensions was possible on the basis of the extensive documentation already mentioned from times when nobody thought of a rebuilding but also because the remains of the building had been thoroughly surveyed and plotted on maps during rubble clearing. In addition to this, old photographs of the exterior and interior of the building were analysed by photographic survey. The unusual quantity of geometrical data thus established and the complicated shape of the building with many single- and double-curved surfaces required the use of modern three-dimensional recording, presentation and planning processes (Fig. 114). Only in this way was the complex planning achievement realized and the demand for complete faithfulness to the original met. Later the planning for use of the sandstone and even its production were carried out by using three-dimensional electronic data processing.

A decisive aspect of archaeological rebuilding was the principle of creating not only the exterior and interior form of the Frauenkirche on a historic basis but also of reproducing entirely the original construction of Bähr's stone building. It was, however, without question that the weaknesses of the preceding building should be avoided and

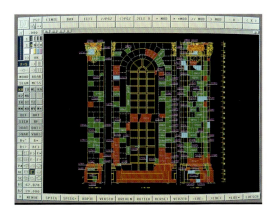

Fig. 119: Computer-aided plotting of the recovered façade stones

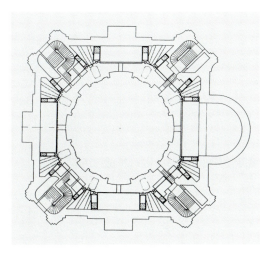

Fig. 118: Frauenkirche, partial layout and isometric design of the tension polygon in the area of the main cornice, office Prof. Wenzel

that today's requirements concerning structural safety should be adopted. The analysis of George Bähr's original construction ideas, the repeatedly needed repairs over 200 years and the original material found during rubble clearance led to important conclusions for the constructional design of the new building. A much higher quality of the newly positioned sandstone, more precise shapes, consistent mortar qualities to meet structural requirements as well as evenly thin joints guarantee double the load-bearing capacity of the building structure compared with the past. This concerns especially the most important load-distributing structural parts like pillars and "spieramen" walls. The assessment of the effective flow of forces in the original cupola building for a long time remained a matter of dispute among engineering scientists and how it might be possible to influence the supporting system in such a way that load distribution from the stone cupola would have no detrimental consequences for the stonework. The concept prepared by the engineering group Wenzel/Jäger embraced the idea of taking up the circumferential tensile strength and the radial thrust at the base of the main cupola by six pre-stressed ring anchors made of high-strength flat steel and forming a polygonal tensile ring in the area of the main cornice. The outward-directed "spieramen" are supported at the rear by strong and safely anchored tie rods (Fig. 118). These modern elements calculated by structural engineering – imitating the principle behind George Bähr's forged iron anchors but meeting more demanding requirements – were meant to compensate for the weaknesses of the supporting frame whose dimensions had, at the time, been calculated intuitively. These construction proposals were countered as late as 1995 in memoranda and in several conferences in which internationally renowned authorities on civil engineering took part, mainly by Professors Siegel, Leonhardt and Zumpe who brought forward completely different solutions which were thoroughly disputed. These solutions bore new risks for the new building by using other building materials or a changed structural principle of action so that – also by reason of progress in building techniques – the previously chosen construction was retained, improved and confirmed by the most thorough structural tests (Fig. 117).

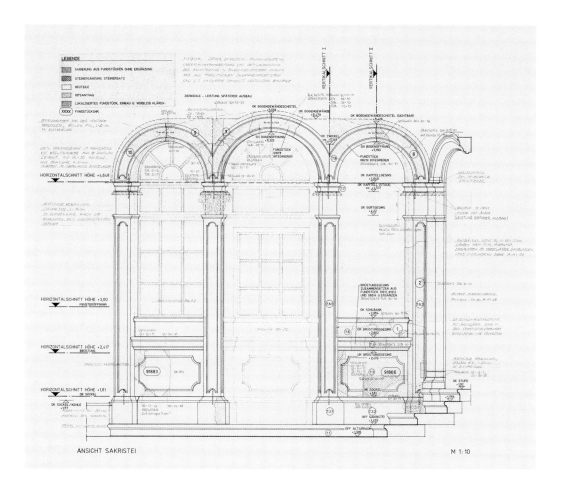

Having answered all basic questions of rebuilding it was possible to continue the planning of the building work and the preparations for the restoration of the sculptural work. The shape of the building had been finally decided upon in the course of "geometrical securing" and presented spatially by means of the 3 D-method. It was now important to start with the precise stone planning for the erection of the building shell and to take into account in the planning work all aspects of further use including safety questions and technical equipment. The building was to become an authentic reconstruction of the old House of God but at the same time it had to meet all indisputable requirements for today's manifold use. The underground exterior building was designed to accommodate cloak rooms, sanitary installations, artists' dressing-rooms and technical supply installations to enable the impressive rooms in the crypt to be used – after the clearing of the old tombs which had been mostly destroyed – as undercroft church, meeting room and memorial place (Fig. 121). New staircases and a lift had to be incorporated to allow handicapped people to

Fig. 120: View drawing of the position of the arches in the area of the sacristy with the inclusion of recovered stones (extract), planning IPRO Dresden

Fig. 121: Frauenkriche, ground plan basement floor with exterior building, drawing IPRO
A undercroft church, B cloak rooms,
C dressing rooms for the orchestra,
D dressing rooms for the choir,
E exhibition, F ventilation, G heating,
H electric installation

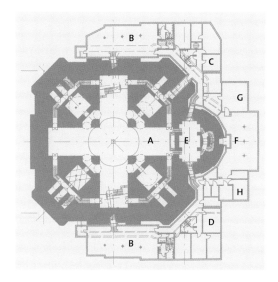

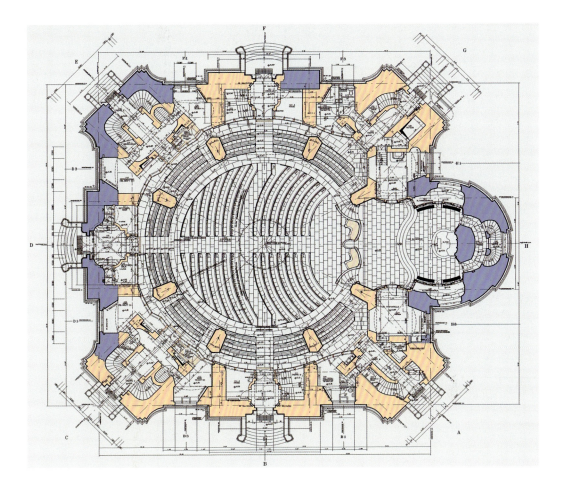

reach these rooms as well as the nave and parts of the galleries. All stairs and accesses had to be designed in accordance with the demands for a safe evacuation of a maximum of 2100 visitors. Fire protection and smoke outlets had also to be taken into account and galleries, balustrades, windows and doors had to be planned in detail. The acoustic conditions in the church had been assessed as outstanding, but the visual relationship and the seating comfort of the visitors had to be improved by more spacious dimensions for the pews. A heating and ventilation plant was set up for the varying permanent use of the church and for constantly guaranteeing air-conditioning in the interior of the church which also suited the building. This plant had to be designed in such a way that the baroque space design, which was true to the original, was visually affected as little as possible. The same concerns affected the design of a modern illumination plant offering the best light conditions for all possible uses and showing the magnificent interior to advantage in its full beauty even without daylight. Safety conditions had to be created for the ascent of tourists in the spiral passage between both cupola shells to the lantern and the covering of the large loft windows towards the cupola with glass was designed to exclude acoustic disturbances during the simultaneous use of the interior space of the church. All these new requirements of an up-to-date rebuilding which yet respected the old model, faced the planning team under Dr. Bernd Kluge, Uwe Kind and Christoph Frenzel with unusual challenges which they were able to meet superbly by exemplary teamwork and with the support of numerous professional partners.

Fig. 122: Ground plan IPRO. The original material which was integrated in the rebuilding is indicated in blue

The years of rebuilding

1992

The rebuilding of the Frauenkirche had been decided but the heap of rubble was still lying untouched and the way to the defined target was blurred. It was not yet clear who could be in overall charge of the huge task, what kind of organizational structures had to be created, in which areas one could start with the preparation work and in which way the whole project could be financed. There were not yet enough competent and potential fellow-workers. The group of supporters for the rebuilding organized a scientific meeting in February 1991 during which the case for an archaeological reconstruction was clearly expressed. On 20th February 1992 the Senior Conservationist Professor Dr. Hans Nadler was able to convince the Dresden Town Council of this and it was decided that the town would support the rebuilding with 10 % of the costs. On this basis the engineering team Wenzel/Jäger was entrusted with the first rough structural calculations, following modern calculation methods and building rules to be able to prove the possibility of rebuilding Bähr's architectural work, reconciling the need to remain true to the original and to make it available for public use. Gradually the other partners for planning and building preparation were found and the Frauenkirche Foundation Dresden e.V. took over the role of the building commissioner. The structural securing of the chancel was carried out by order of the town with the help of sponsored scaffolding (Fig. 125); the planning office IPRO was responsible for analysing all existing documents and deciding what equipment would be needed on the construction site. The definite preparations for the archaeological rubble clearing were the first step in the rebuilding work.

1993

With the opening ceremony of the construction site on both sides of the Landhausstrasse on 12th February 1993 and the installation of the first tower crane it was possible to continue intensively the rubble clearing which had already started in January under well thought-out working conditions. At the same time the orderly site, visible from all sides with its containers, sheds and storage racks for the stones were the best advertisement for the project.

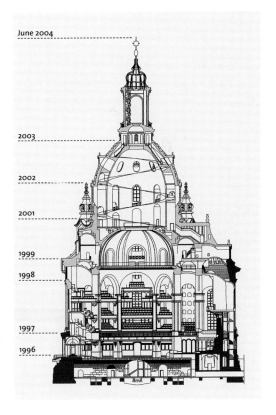

The site offices and staff rooms for the management, building supervisors, engineering teams and the participating firms were accommodated in a two-floor building – for a short time, also, an exhibition room with information material on

Fig. 123: Stone head of the staircase tower G in the heap of rubble where it had collapsed, condition 1945

Fig. 124: Annual growth of the rebuilding from 1996 to 2004

Fig. 125: Chancel area with scaffolding for securing work, 1992

Fig. 126: Construction site with revolving tower cranes, December 1993

the Frauenkirche which soon had to be replaced, for reasons of space, by its own pavilion. After the early attempts to find the right working method, the archaeological rubble clearing soon got going and brought to light more and more precious original pieces which were analysed scientifically and measured technologically right on site. The relative position of the pieces found in the heap of rubble was photographically documented from the cabin of the crane over an area of 71×74 m. Especially spectacular was the recovery of coherent big pieces coming from staircase towers, the masonry of the cupola or from pillars, whose assessment and re-use were keenly disputed (Fig. 123). Besides stones there were found thousands of other pieces providing information on the history and destruction of the church – among them were candle holders and the altar crucifix, bits of furnishings, rails and handrails, remains of wooden parts of the interior, pieces of glass from windows, lamps, metal fittings and locks, forged-iron reinforcements in the stonework, steel bands from pillars, twisted steel girders from the galleries, parts of the heating installation, even tools and materials of the craftsmen or undamaged rolls of film from the film archives of the "Reich", which had been stored in the basement (Fig. 127). It was a lucky stroke of fate that the old cross from the top of the church – although badly twisted – could be recovered from the rubble (Fig. 128). Besides charred pieces of documents, well-preserved coins from the time when it was built were found in its orb and these were later put into the new orb. The exposure of the altar behind its protective wall in October was awaited with eager expectation. It showed less damage than had been feared. The organ gallery which had fallen down, soon after the fire, had destroyed the upper projecting parts of the altar front but the charred wooden parts had cushioned the force of the stone blocks when the choir vault collapsed and thus had protected those parts which had been knocked off and the undamaged remains of the relief from complete destruction. This created the obligatory challenge to recover painstakingly almost 2000 pieces of rubble from the altar for reconstruction (Fig. 129) so as to be able to show to even greater advantage in the new church this most precious and meaningful part of the original interior fittings. By the end of the year rubble clearing was finished by using a mobile excavator and suction technology for the debris so that the remaining masonry could be measured for planning the building work. The first ceremonial Christmas evensong on 23rd December 1993 in the cleared ruin in front of the remains of the altar was an impressive symbol of gratitude and hope.

Fig. 127: Uncovered, mainly undamaged instructional films of the former Air Ministry of the German Reich

Fig. 128: Recovery of the cross of the cupola on 1st July 1993

Fig. 129: Recovered fragments from the area of the altar

Fig. 130: View into the cleared ruin, 1994

1994

Archaeological rubble clearing lasted until May of that year and within only 17 months about 22000 m³ of rubble were removed and scientifically analysed (Fig. 130). Comprehensive information on the building history, construction engineering, geometry and materials used, ageing and damage by the environment as well as the collapse of the building on 15th February 1945 was obtained and could now be used for the planning of the rebuilding work. The Frauenkirche Foundation wanted to take practical steps towards rebuilding and give visible signs to the public. The first experimental reconstruction of the top of a staircase tower was prepared and carried out as a kind of test model for the archaeological rebuilding. Five parts from the base of the northwest staircase tower were recovered in the heap of rubble in relatively well preserved condition. They were cleaned and documented and repaired with stone. Missing sculptured parts were re-carved and fitted in, e.g. the "egg basket", the shaft of the centre-piece, the flame vase and others (Fig. 131). The successful result convinced the experts and made clear to the site management how to proceed further. For the sculpturing work it was decided to use only the hard and weather-resistant Cotta sandstone ("weisse Bank") which – thanks to its close-grained texture – is suitable for sculpting. It was also decided that for the repair of recovered pieces only old material of the same type should be used and that the use of mortar as stone replacement should be excluded because it does not develop a blackish patina and subsequently would show a speckled stone surface. Even for the preparation of normal ashlars from the rubble material various stonecutting firms were asked to submit test pieces which were thoroughly assessed and subjected to material tests. On the basis of these results it was possible to work out binding conditions for submitting tenders for the reconstructions of recovered stones as far as repair technology, joint and surface design were concerned, involving skilled craftsmanship. At the same time it was decided to establish in the immediate vicinity of the church a working area with sheds for the stonemasons and a sawing workshop Figs. 115/132). The time-honoured work practice of the masons' guilds had thus been revived.

Fig. 131: Top of a staircase tower as test reconstruction in the area of the stone storage yard

Fig. 132: Reconstruction of a recovered piece in the stonemasons' shed Neumarkt, a stonemason is preparing the insertion of squarestones

The actual rebuilding work started after careful preparation on 27th May with the public act of positioning the 1st stone at the southeast wall between entrance A and the chancel (Fig. 133). This was the place in which it was intended to test the positioning techniques, the making of the joints and various mortar mixtures. The experts decided to apply the traditional method: to position the dry stones on a rolled lead strip, then apply a brick backing at a distance of 1 to 2 metres, close the joints with hemp rope and finally fill them with liquid mortar (Fig. 134). This method was adhered to until the stonework was completed.

The experience gained in completing this test section and during the following months showed that the lifting accuracy of tower cranes was not sufficient for carrying out precise positioning work, that the existing ruins as well as the fresh masonry positioned on them needed weather protection and that the working techniques needed to be improved to reduce costs. Solutions had to be found for these problems.

In order to create ground clearance for the erection of the planned exterior building, archaeological excavations were started for the investigation and rescuing of valuable traces of the town's history on the land where the old Frauenkirche cemetery and the former Materni hospital had stood. The rich finds of burial places, jewellery, tombstones and a well still containing water in the area of the hospital again made clear the historic importance of this place (Fig. 135).

At the end of the year the Dresden Frauenkirche Foundation – founded in June by the Free State of Saxony, the Saxon Lutheran Church and the town of Dresden as commissioner for the rebuilding and the further preservation of the Frauenkirche – was operational after having appointed its management with Eberhard Burger as director. It was in the position to direct the building work closely and successfully give it publicity for obtaining private and public money.

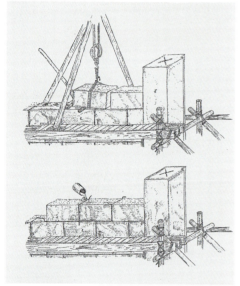

Fig. 133: Laying of the first stone at entrance A

Fig. 134: Historic technique of positioning an ashlar, drawing by Torsten Remus

Fig. 135: Excavations in the area of the cemetery of the Frauenkirche

Fig. 136: Exposed and repaired foundations of the church; working on the bottom slab of the exterior building

1995

The excavation for the exterior building was prepared after the archaeological rescue work had been concluded and made watertight by permanently lowering the water table. Now the exposed church foundations had to be surveyed and restored to check the structural assumptions, because the historic joint mortar had not been strong enough during the building work in the winter of 1726/27 (Fig. 136). The new underground functional section was built as a watertight "white trough" made of pre-stressed concrete and separated from the main building by an expansion joint running around it. The connecting openings, leading to the church cellars through the 4.5 m thick masonry of the foundation, were made by means of diamond rope saws and covered with shotcrete. It was possible to use the exterior building for site purposes as soon as the shell of the building was finished, all the more so, because the work was now concentrated on the completion of the basement walls for the new vault. The first thing to be done was to carry out a survey to make sure that no displacements or tilting had taken place in the area of the foundations as a result of the collapse of the building which would have had critical consequences for the rebuilding work. There was a positive result to tests also carried out on the bracings between the crossing piers installed by Bähr and the main arches under the ring of pillars brought in by Rüth for the securing of the foundations (Fig. 137). Two new stairways were built for public use of the undercroft and ventilation and cable ducts were installed in the basement floor. The main measuring points from the time of the first building could be found in the central point of the church and under the chancel (Fig. 138). The careful logging of damage, the subsequent planning of the restoration measures and the preparation of the connecting masonry for the new barrel vault were especially time-consuming. The prefabricated stones for the vault were recovered from the old material reclaimed during rubble clearing and from the stones from the demolition of the historic Torgau Elbe bridge – a significant combination of materials for the Frauenkirche memorial! The first section of the vaults was started before the winter. The damaged upper masonry of the exterior walls and the destroyed pillar bases were removed down to the level where rebuilding would start. It was very inconvenient and time-consuming to open the temporary weather-protection cover each time the crane was used. A solution was found which meant that rails for the crane were installed on strengthened scaffolding supports under the protective roof. A gantry crane with a smoothly controllable crane carriage could run on these rails (Fig. 141). Thanks to this lifting technology it was also possible to

Fig. 137: Foundation slab between the crossing piers from the time of the original construction

Fig. 138: The point of the historic marking peg in the centre of the church

Fig. 139: Altar. Attaching and pinning of broken off parts of the capitals to the main body; gilding and colouring preserved in large parts

Fig. 140: Altar fragment with temporary securing of parts in danger of collapse

Fig. 141: First gantry crane with crane carriage under the temporary weather protection roof

Fig. 142: View into the main space of the undercroft after having closed the vault

work more precisely and effectively during the erection of the second test section on the exterior wall of entrance C and a constant quality could be ensured, even in winter weather, by using foil cladding and heating in the area.

Emergency safety work on the parts of the altar which were in danger of collapse had been carried out. It followed an extensive logging of the damage to consider possible technical steps for a restoration of the stones (Fig. 140). Simultaneously restorers investigated for the first time the very informative traces of the historic colouring of the altar and produced preliminary studies on the colouring of the church interior (Fig. 139).

1996

In spite of the hard winter the vaulting of the main cellar was carried out according to plan but the work for fitting in the stones up to the level of the first encircling horizontal joint and in the spandrels was extremely time-consuming. Again and again connection dimensions had to be determined, according to which the new stones were prepared in the sawing house or had to be attached on the spot. The even positioning of the moulded stones in the Gothic bond (two runners, one binder alternatively) went even faster on the movable supporting framework so that by May the keystone (Fig. 143) was positioned at the crossing point of the barrels. It was immensely impressive when, after the vault masonry was in place, the shuttering was lowered and removed and for the first time it was possible to appreciate the width of the large room and the regularity of the stone cutting. About 5600 stones had been positioned. With the consecration of the completed undercroft by Bishop Volker Kreß in August the explicit meaning of the building became clear and the agreed principle of simultaneous "using and building" was implemented (Fig. 144). Numerous rebuilding concerts, divine services, lectures and guided tours were organized although nine years of building work had still to be carried out on the site.

A syndicate of firms was entrusted with the first building work above the surface of the ground up to the window sills and in May the rebuilding work started. It was possible to rely on the experience gained from the two trial runs and on the improved abilities of the stonemasons and bricklayers. It was a great achievement to obtain such an even structure from the original stones, repaired pieces of rubble and new material by the old, and nowadays unusual, surface treatment. The change in lifting techniques from a tower crane to the more easily controlled gantry cranes with crane carriages, the erection of a heated "tent" around the church as well as well-established stone technology produced a very effective building process.

Fig. 143: Inserting the key stone in the main vault

Fig. 144: Consecration of the undercroft church on 21st August 1996

Fig. 145: Lifting of the protective roof 1997 and the six positions of the protective roof

1997

The completion of the lower wall section up to a height of 8.10 m on 11th April was a clear success for all partners – George Bähr's impressive architecture with the curved walls, the portals and the beautifully profiled belt course could once again be admired. However the hard winter required a great effort for the tempering of the ashlars in preheating chambers to guarantee a constant stability of the masonry. The next contracts were given to four firms already working on the site to begin construction of the shell building up to a height of 16.40 m within 16 months. The work included the exterior masonry in the area of the windows, the interior pillars and the galleries, i. e. highly demanding work for which the protective roof would have to be dismantled and raised. Luckily, the work-team entrusted with this task had found a better and less time-consuming solution. The roof frame was reinforced and stabilized to lift the weight of 270 tons to the next position by means of hydraulic lifters resting on special hoisting supports (Fig. 145). Extreme load differences were compensated by the mobile crane operating in parallel and only three days were needed for the height to be raised by 10.5 m. Parts of the ruin were still visible above the housing but the operational height was sufficient to erect the eight enormous pillars in the interior. These pillars had to fulfil the highest requirements concerning stone quality, accuracy in measurement and mortar quality because of their important load-bearing function (Fig. 146).

The best, homogeneous sandstone material had already been chosen in the quarry; it was then tested in the laboratory and once more visually assessed before cutting it in the Saxon sandstone works. The stones were allowed to have a tolerance of only 2 mm after having been surface-treated by the craftsmen. They were at first positioned in a dry state on the site to be checked and then set up to form a pillar with exactly calculated joints (Fig. 147). Thanks to the constantly growing response to the rebuilding work and the growing number of donors all eight pillars of the interior could be financed by Dresdner Bank Donors' Certificates.

Fig. 146: View into the interior with choir pillar A

Fig. 147: Setting of a pillar stone

1998

In this year work was continued up to a height of about 20 m – the arches of the windows and the pilaster capitals were completed with many recovered pieces (Fig. 148). Behind the façade the stairwells, wall sections, "spieramen" and spandrels had reached the fourth gallery (Fig. 149). The protective roof was raised to a height of 33.5 m and now covered the whole church including the remaining ruins which were integrated into the growing masonry by means of pre-stressed anchors. The work of the carpenters and masons to make the conic vaulting above the inner window embrasures was demanding and good practice for the ever more complicated vault shapes in the upper sections of the church. As for the much disputed question of what to do with the parts of the west gables which had collapsed at the destruction of the church, the Foundation Council decided against the preservation of the remaining rubble in the ground in front of entrance D as a permanent memorial. In the Autumn the fragments were taken apart and 76 reclaimed ashlars were positioned in the new building with almost 10 m³ of backing stones (Fig. 150). The new bell-carrying frame was erected on the spot where these fragments had been. The bell of the old Frauenkirche from 1518 was temporarily brought into use in this frame (Fig. 151). It had been in Hubertusburg palace since 1925 and survived the war without damage. It became part of the new set of bells in 2003.

Fig. 149: View from above into the church interior with the completed pillars and the so-called "bee-hives" at the side of the choir, 1998

Fig. 150: Taking apart the big piece fallen from the west gable

Fig. 148: Façade section of staircase tower A with original stones in the new masonry

Fig. 151: The new bell-carrying frame on the site in front of the church near Münzgasse

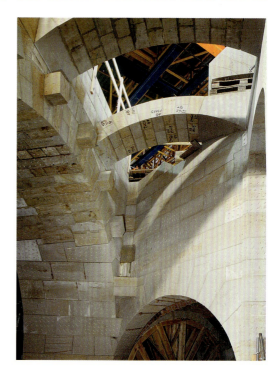

Fig. 152: Supporting framework for the arches between the main pillars

Fig. 153: Arcature above staircase A

1999

In March a building stage was reached which had been planned for the end of the year, i.e. the work was nine months ahead of schedule and promised that the exterior church building would be completed before the end of 2004. The difficult negotiations for the placing of contracts for the building work, including the positioning of the orb and cross, were conducted bearing this in mind and the envisaged cost structure was accepted. However, the work to be done was extremely demanding and had to be carefully prepared. A roofed floor had to be designed for the carpenters at the west side where the supporting framework for the large spandrels between the interior pillars was manufactured and then put together on the spot (Fig. 152). Extremely complicated, spherically curved geometrical requirements placed the highest demands on supporting framework construction, stone planning and positioning techniques, needed for the building of the four arched crossings above each pillar head – two to the neighbouring pillars and two to the "spieramen" (Fig. 153). Finding the right shape for the individual ashlars and their accurate preparation in the sandstone works would not have been possible without a computer. All those involved did a great job. The work of the craftsmen 260 years ago, who had achieved such good results with much simpler means, was more and more admired. After having completed the arches, the various vault caps above the marginal zones of the church space were bricked up and the groin vaults were installed whose wall connections were difficult and never uniform; these were put in above the galleries provided for singers additional to the choir.

The widespread coffered vault above the entrance axes B, D and F were started at the end of the year and the exterior masonry reached about 26.5 m. Each day up to 19 m³ of sandstone was brought to the site on four trucks, positioned and many reconstructed recovered pieces were fitted. In this way both old and new were connected without concealing the scars and deformations from the destruction (Fig. 154). In the meantime the restorers had been successful with the reconstruction of the pieces recovered from the church interior behind a protective wall at the altar and the sculptor Vincenz Wanitschke had finished a new stuccoed model of the descending angel (Fig. 65).

Fig. 154: Connection of the window arch to the remains of the ruin of staircase tower E, which during destruction had leaned outward

2000

The vaulted pillar arches were raised around the building up until the interior cornice was reached. This ring of the cupola base, with a width of 2.2 m, forms the main load-bearing member for load distribution from the inner and main cupola to the pillars in the interior, the "spieramen" and the wall areas towards the exterior wall. It had to be built with special care (Fig. 156).

On 13th February the Duke of Kent handed over the remade orb and cross during a religious ceremony. It had been forged as a sign of reconciliation and as a donation by the British Dresden Trust in London and was a facsimile of the destroyed original. As a shining symbol of the new fraternal community under the cross and amidst the rejoicing of thousands of people, it was lifted by a crane over the weather protection roof up to the future height of 95 m and then temporarily set up in front of the church.

The main cornice running round the church was completed layer by layer to complete the façade; the individual parts had a weight of more than 5 tons and therefore had to be lifted in by a mobile swing crane through openings in the protective roof. The protrusion of about 1 m over the exterior wall had to be secured against tilting by supports on the façade scaffolding (Fig. 158). The platform for carrying out work on the curved base of the cupola had to be lifted again in May to a height of 45 m. This was done within a few hours thanks to good technological preparation. It was then possible to erect the shell vault of the choir on a perfect formwork under the best possible site conditions (Fig. 155). The steel tension ring around the curved cupola base, allowing an even load distribution of the cupola forces to the lower supporting elements and leaving the masonry free from cracks, was installed in June (Fig. 157).

All shuttering and supporting framework used for the vaulting work had to be removed in the autumn to create a space free from scaffolding for the first events in December. Only the central scaffold was still standing on which the supporting ceiling above the cornice was resting. It was meant to carry the preparation floor for the vaulting of the inner cupola. A temporary wooden floor had to be installed in the nave as well as landings and rails on the galleries for the divine services during Advent and the Christmas season (Fig. 10).

Fig. 156: The finished lower cornice above the pillar arches

Fig. 157: Installation of the polygonal steel tension ring

Fig. 158: Setting of a large ashlar in the main cornice by means of a mobile crane

Fig. 155: Completed choir vault above the altar

Fig. 159: Starting to vault the inner cupola on the supporting framework

Fig. 160: Completed inner cupola, curved cupola base with flying buttresses and area of the dormer windows in the staircase towers

2001

The vaulting of the inner cupola was the main work in the first half of January, initially totally in sandstone and then in the upper area divided into sandstone ribs and masonry sections (Fig. 159). A grand cupola celebration was held by the site team after the profiled pressure ring around the cupola opening and the dismantling of the supporting framework had been completed. The vertical masonry ring with the hollow passageway and the radial stiffening flying buttresses were built parallel to the lower part of the cupola. This section stretches to the first tambour cornice of the main cupola and contains the large dormer windows in the curved base of the cupola. Stone bosses for the later positioning of the cover slabs were integrated in the flying buttresses (Fig. 160). Flat brick arches were inserted between these ribs to ensure a joint-free seal over the whole surface of the substructure under the stone roof which can reliably be drained even with concealed rain pipes. This complicated design should in the future exclude water damage at the base of the cupola which constantly appeared in the original building (Fig. 161).

In the meantime the upper vaults for access to future ascent to the cupola were built in the chancel. The staircase towers with their especially sophisticated forms for the arched bell chambers, dormer windows, oval windows and roofing were continuously growing upwards. With the spectacular use of a giant mobile swing crane it was possible accurately to position the recovered 75 ton so-called "butterfly" on top of the upper room in staircase tower G – a truly masterly feat of engineering technology (Fig. 162). The work on the exterior had to be accelerated because the dismantling of the façade scaffolding was planned for 2002; this included the installation of the stone bars for the windows and the installation of the novel multi-shell glasswork in steel frames. These windows can in some places be opened to let out smoke and let in fresh air. Besides that, all plumbing work for roof drainage and the covering of cornices with copper sheeting had to be carried out. At the beginning of September a 6 m wide test section on pillar F was covered with plaster, dry masonry, stucco and colouring from the base of the pillar up to the cornice of the inner cupola as a trial run for future interior refurbishment (Fig. 61).

Fig. 161: Inserting the brick arches between the flying buttresses with stone bosses for the cover slabs

Fig. 162: The so-called "butterfly", which was recovered from the rubble – having a weight of 75 tons, is back in its former position crowning staircase tower G

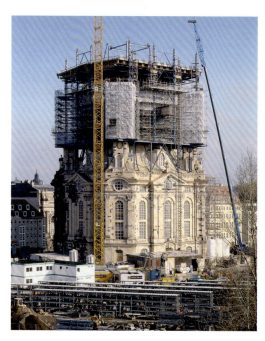

Fig. 163: Working on the cupola masonry in the vertical tambour zone

Fig. 164: Tensioning of the first tensioning ring in the area of the facing balustrade of the tambour zone

Fig. 165: South west view after having dismantled the main scaffolding when lifting the weather-protection roof Above the scaffolding of the cupola

2002

New and smaller scaffolding for the erection of the outer cupola above the main cornice was installed around the turn of the year. The rib-like substructure of the chancel roof was brought up above the vaults similar to the flying buttresses. The curved base of the cupola was at first covered with the special cover stones (Fig. 184) and the covering of the roof of the chancel was carried out in April after which the weather protection roof was shortened and lifted to the new working height of 57 m. The roof connections and covers in the area of the cupola base were then fitted with rolled lead which harmonizes better than copper with the dark patina of sandstone. The vertical masonry area of the tambour zone of the cupola could now be started (Fig. 163). The complex cross section of the two-shell cupola construction with the intermediate ribs and the beginning of the spiral ramp leading to the viewing platform had to be built. During this work two of the six ring anchors were installed at the same time. With the increasing load during the ongoing work they were pre-stressed and later covered with ashlars and grouted (Fig. 164).

Plasterers, stucco-workers, dry construction workers, steelworkers and other technical professions worked in the interior. This put heavy demands on the planning of the work in the interior and required close coordination. The side installations in the choir area for the confessional boxes, the sacristy and the baptistery took on their shape using recovered stones. The test section (Fig. 61) was ready for analysis in May. Nine artists submitted samples for the painting of the inner cupola.

The main scaffolding was dismantled in the summer and in the middle of September the reconstructed stonework became visible in its impressive unity up to the main cornice, the triangular gables and the curved cupola base with the large vertical dormer windows (Fig. 165). The main cupola was built behind the protective housing up to the middle of the lower dormer windows where the tilt towards the interior gradually starts and a backing is required. About 400 m³ of sandstone material were used each month for the building of the cupola. A supporting framework in the form of an ellipsoid was erected for the vaulting work. It was installed on a supporting grid and represented a unique piece of art in accuracy and perfect finish (Fig. 166). For a last time the weather protection roof was lifted in November under problematic weather conditions and the housing was extended to ensure building could continue in winter until the exterior cupola was completed in May 2003.

Fig. 166: Carpenters during work on the supporting framework of the main cupola

Fig. 167:
Installation of the lantern top with orb and cross

Fig. 168:
Freely visible main cupola with scaffold for the lantern construction site

2003

The cupola was continuously growing in outstanding quality thanks to improving preparation and preheating of the stone materials on pallets for the corresponding working section. At first the 25 cm thick inner shell was made of standard stones positioned in a circle against the supporting framework; at the same time the cross ribs with the arches for the spiral passage were built up. After that the back wall of the 1.2 to 2.2 m thick outer shell and the supporting vaults under the spiral ramp were completed on inserted framework sections. Finally the large copings were positioned in a dry condition and grouted with mortar with a low degree of shrinkage. The building of the staircase towers A and C was finished in February.

Fig. 169: Positioning of the decorative upper part of the flame vase on staircase tower G

The work in the interior of the church was in full swing on all levels. A lot of time was needed for the galleries because of fire protection, the laying of cables and the subsequent work of the carpenters and stucco-workers. Floors and staircases had to be made of sandstone in many areas. Arcatures for the sacristy, the baptistery and the confessional boxes in the choir area were completed; restorers worked on the altar while stucco-work was carried out on the capitals of the pillars and in the inner cupola. When the stonework in the staircase towers E and G was finished, the carpenters erected bell cages of excellent quality because the new bells were due to arrive in Dresden in a festive procession and to be consecrated in May. During Whitsuntide the great peal of bells rang out for the first time with a crowd of people listening with great feeling.

At the end of June the uppermost stepped layers of the outer cupola were positioned and the last ring anchor was tensioned. The supporting framework was dismantled and the celebration for the main cupola was held in the high-vaulted cupola on 1st July. The erection of the lantern neck on top of the cupola was started and the final work on the exterior of the surfaces of the cupola was carried out, i.e. jointing, installation of the window bars, sheet metal covering and lightning protection. After having positioned the last flame vases on the staircase towers (Fig. 169) it was possible to dismantle the scaffolding of the main cupola together with the lower supporting grid. The connecting openings at the tambour and in the base of the cupola were closed. The completed cupola was now towering above the ground and visible from far away (Fig. 168). The building site for the lantern was provided with its own weather protection enclosure and an additional staircase above the roof of the chancel. Before finally positioning the protective roof for the lantern it was necessary carefully to remove, by means of the tower crane, the dismantled steel girders of the inner scaffolding through the centric openings. After that the building was prepared for the winter and slowly heated for the other professions working inside as well as for the demanding work on the lantern at a height of 70 m.

2004

In this year all energy was concentrated on the well-planned continuation of the work in the interior demanding the highest qualifications in all professions and perfect coordination among them. The new pipe scaffolding in the interior of the main cupola was used for coating the surface with plaster, painting the walls, installing the electrical equipment, plastering the walls of the spiral ramp and laying sandstone slabs on its floor. The large window panes between the ramp and the cupola space were fitted without frames in the plaster work and windows were installed by the steelworkers in the dormers of the cupola.

The stonework of the lantern was finished in April. It made the highest demands on those who planned and completed the work because the sandstone in the lantern shafts had to have three dressed sides and had to be made and positioned with great precision. No old reclaimed stone pieces were used because only homogenous stone material was suited for reasons of high structural requirements to cope with extreme wind strengths occurring at this height. Tensioned anchors had to be installed in the slender shafts for safety reasons. A cassette with documents on the rebuilding work was inserted in the lantern cornice when the keystone was

ceremonially laid. After that the place where the lantern roof rested had to be prepared. Meanwhile the roof framing for the lantern was erected by the carpenters on the ground in front of the church. Its parts had been manufactured in a Dresden apprentices' training shop. They had now to be joined together by modern steel connections because traditional craftsman-style mortising is nowadays not permissible for such tasks. There were especially high-quality requirements for the covering of the bulbous dome with copper on a framework to guarantee durability over generations. Discrete spotlights were installed around the lantern top to illuminate the church at night. Finally the new cross was connected with the "Kaiserstab" in the centre of the top and two capsules with documents were placed in the orb. The top of the lantern was positioned by means of a high crane at a festive ceremony with a divine service in the presence of about 60 000 people on 22nd June. With this the exterior building of the church was completed (Fig. 167).

A revolving scaffold under the inner cupola was used for carrying out the architectural painting and the ceiling paintings in the panels of the cupola as well as the gilding (Fig. 170). The interior scaffold was gradually dismantled after the paintwork in the church had been finished to allow the ground floor to be covered with sandstone. The floor heating, ventilating ducts and illumination equipment on the galleries were installed, the three-ply larch floor was laid and treated with a hard wax oil. The wooden inner doors and windows were installed and the entire walkway to the lantern was completed by the end of the year. The precision work of restorers, sculptors and gilders on the altar and the organ front was continued in the chancel sheltered by scaffolds and tarpaulins. A first impression of the festive effect of the church space was given after the installation of the choir screen and the pulpit and the completion of the paintwork.

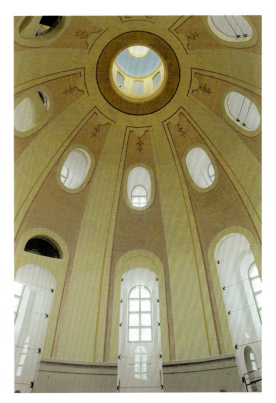

Fig. 171: Main cupola space with arch and oval openings after having finished painting work

Fig. 172: View of exterior door A

Fig. 170: View into the inner cupola with the revolving scaffold during painting work

Fig. 173: Assembly of the pipes in the organ front

Fig. 174: Lifting in of the wooden pipes

Fig. 175: Action and roller board of the great organ during assembly

2005

In Spring the area around the church was prepared, the outer doors – excellent masterpieces by young carpenters (Fig. 172) – were installed and the access to the viewing platform was opened to visitors. 900 to 1700 visitors came daily to enjoy the unparalleled, beautiful panorama over the roofs of the city into the Elbe valley and on their way up got a first sight of the interior of the cupola (Fig. 171). With their entrance fees they helped to finance the remaining work in the interior.

The paintings in the cupola were skilfully completed by Christoph Wetzel and accepted and praised by a jury of experts. The revolving scaffold was dismantled after the gilding work had been finished and the coloured forged iron railing on the lower cornice was completed. The illumination equipment was also installed in this area. The restorers finished the colouring and gilding work on the altar front. The paintings in the side rooms behind the choir arcades were finished and equipment was installed in them. The choir screen with the confessional boxes arranged in front of it was decorated with wooden carvings. After the completion of the organ gallery and the richly decorated organ front it was possible to install the new organ by David Kern of Strasbourg (Fig. 173–175). Before he could start with the tuning of the instrument without construction noise and dust in August, it was necessary to complete the benches in the nave, all doors and private prayer boxes and the sound transmission equipment with the sound studio. The exterior south building was changed after use by the construction workers to fulfil its final functions of providing a general cloakroom, sanitary facilities, cloakrooms for the singers and changing rooms for the admission personnel. Tests for the multiple use of the building were started in October after the tuning of the organ had been finished and the preparations for the ceremonial re-consecration of this House of God on 30th October could be started.

A magnificent teamwork of planners and builders, scientists, curators of monuments, restorers and artists and many promoters of the building work in Germany and all over the world has reached its ceremonial completion – and, just as in the time of the first builders, the dedication is "Soli Deo Gloria" – solely to the Glory of God (Fig. 176).

Fig. 176:
Crowning of the organ front with cartouche S.D.G. – "Soli Deo Gloria"

Fig. 177:
Keyboard and organ frontal
The layout of the playing desk is based in form and colour on playing facilities for organs created by Gottfried Silbermann, but it is in this case a reconstruction

Fig. 178: View into the undercroft church with altar created by Anish Kapor and chairs

Specific features of the rebuilding – a monument and its active use

Fig. 179: Undercroft, room with tombstones, chapel G. Design of the tomb chapels by Michael Schoenholtz

The theoretical principles of archaeological rebuilding were known to all participants of the Frauenkirche project over the years of planning and building as theoretical guidelines, but putting them into practice again and again became a difficult tightrope to walk between a strict rebuilding which was true to the original from a conservationist's point of view and the necessary adaptation to meet the functional, constructional and safety requirements for an up-to-date multi-purpose church. From the very beginning there was no doubt that the rebuilding should be orientated as far as possible to George Bähr's type and system of construction and that the shortcomings and weaknesses of the historic building should be corrected in the light of today's knowledge to preserve the monument by using it. However, where did the optimum compromise lie in each individual case which required concessions on all sides? On one occasion the justified interests of the users dominated, on another the opinion of the conservationists and restorers, however, the scientifically based engineering arguments prevailed in almost all cases when structural interests were concerned. Vehement debates were held on various disputed plans, primarily among specialists and sometimes very emotionally in public, which in some cases led to misunderstandings and offence.

Today's extended function of the church as a place for the most varied forms of divine service and other church events, as a memorial, concert hall, reconciliation centre and tourist attraction goes far beyond what the original building had to provide. Solutions could be found for most of the multiple tasks which did not violate the historic heritage and which respected its inherent rules. The conversion of the crypt, no longer used

as a burial ground, into the undercroft was a great advantage, allowing the reconstruction of the impressive historic areas and the addition of the necessary constructional amendments in today's architectural style (Fig. 178). After the consecration of the Frauenkirche it is used as a sacred area of tranquillity, around which the burial vaults are arranged diagonally and used as places of memorial. Symbolistic sculptures by Michael Schoenholz are displayed there and, together with relics from old burial grounds, give these rooms an impressive character which should inspire visitors (Figs. 179).

This extension of use only became possible by the new exterior building in which all rooms required for visitors, event management and technical equipment were accommodated, which otherwise would have filled the basement of the church. Additional sanitary facilities for the individual floors were discreetly arranged in the small rooms beside the staircases.

Measures to allow use by handicapped persons were taken at staircase G without impairing the original building structure. The new pews were designed with more space between the benches to provide more comfort, however in the nave they were arranged in fixed blocks as it was in the original building, although moveable seating for different occasions would have been practical to cope with the stream of tourists as well as many groups of visitors. The reconstruction of the choir balustrade with the central pulpit lectern and the stairs rising at the sides was disputed for a long time because concerts with large choirs would need precisely this area to take into account contemporary concepts and the acoustic conditions of the Frauenkirche, the view to the altar would be obstructed by installations and a broad, open flight of stairs to the choir would have facilitated religious use (Fig. 180). In this case the approach of the conservationists to the authentic realization of Bähr's perception of space was implemented while the high pulpit installed on the left choir pillar by Feige in 1739 was not rebuilt although many fragments had been recovered and it would have been part of the complete historic spatial image (Fig. 181).

The use of the Frauenkirche by tourists, which in former times did not exist in today's numbers, required a few additional partitions, mainly to organize the stream of visitors to the viewing platform without danger and disturbance for simultaneous performances in the church interior. This included large panes of glass being inserted in the light apertures of the main cupola, which

Fig. 181: Pulpit by Johann Christian Feige on the northeast Choir pillar, photograph, after 1904

served as sound insulation and smoke protection for the spiral ramp (Fig. 182), sound-proofing doors, but also a lift in the tower G staircase and sufficiently wide, safe stairs in the area of the choir roof and the lantern access.

The structurally based changes to the load-bearing system are of great importance. George Bähr had designed it correctly but probably on intuition but for various reasons, the changes could not be implemented completely without causing damage. The installation of six pre-stressed ring anchors under the top layer of the main cupola was a modern addition which nevertheless corresponded with the historic construction with forged anchor components. Completely new and long disputed was the installation of the polygonal tension ring on the level of the main cornice (Fig. 183) to which paired tension rods were connected taking up the radial downward thrusting forces from the load of the cupola to the "spieramen" by means of strong

Fig. 180: Choir with the axial arrangement of pulpit, baptismal font, altar and organ

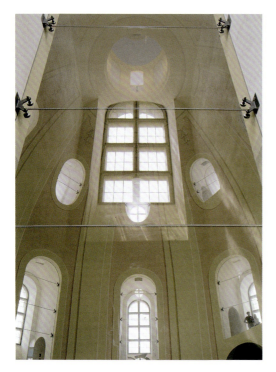

construction of the lantern top and the anchoring of the lantern stems. The problem of weatherproofing and durability of the outer shell of the cupola had been long and controversially discussed among the planners and clients. The shell solution chosen for the cupola base and the roof of the chancel is new for the stone building and still must prove its effectiveness and, if necessary, could be replaced by another type of sealing (Fig. 184).

All these changes compared with the original building structure are based on today's much higher safety requirements and severe building regulations, especially for such public assembly places. The skill and ingenuity of the planners and builders meant that these changes did not have any visible effect on the outer appearance of the reconstructed Frauenkirche. It is, however, necessary to ask, if the term "archaeological rebuilding" in the case of the Frauenkirche still reflects the entire reality of this admirable work created in our time.

head blocks and diverting it into the vertical. This ensuring of the originally planned load flux was necessary in the view of the planners' of the load-bearing system and of the test engineers to exclude permanently cracks and settlement in the building. The "spieramen" masonry was additionally reinforced with horizontal stainless steel anchors. In addition more detailed decisions concerning stone quality and the structure of the masonry, joint configuration and mortar quality were taken, largely improving the structural safety in load transfer. In some cases it was decided against the re-use of historically significant pieces of rubble – so-called major fragments –, which would have been important to conservationists as "relics" and evidence of the destruction. There prevailed worries that the material properties were too different compared with the new material as former repair measures had shown and thus could provoke damage to the building.

The galleries which have a complicated spatial form were rebuilt with adequate safety as pure steel structures (Fig. 185). The old wooden galleries had had to be strengthened with steel girders in the 1930s. Also the ceiling above the inner cupola, the front of the private prayer boxes and other components were constructed and clad with steel elevations to reduce the fire risk. Today's specifications have also determined the

Fig. 182: Fixed glazing in the inner shell of the cupola separates the passage for the visitors in the spiral ramp leading to the lantern platform from the church interior

Fig. 183: Steel tension ring and "spieramen" anchor

Fig. 184: Cover slabs of the curved cupola base on the masonry projections in front of the south dormer window in the curved base of the cupola

The high fire-protection requirements already mentioned, in many places affect the width of doors, entrances and exits to guarantee safe evacuation, but the visitor will hardly notice this deviation from the historic original. Modern smoke alarms, smoke outlets in the windows and in the upper opening of the cupola, smoke-tight doors and glazing in the staircases or the glass insulation of the ascent to the lantern against the cupola are more visible interferences in the original building. The fire-proof insulation of the steel galleries with the accommodation of the ducts for heating and ventilation as well as illumination was a very laborious task and avoided an unjustifiable oversimplification of the original specifications of the components.

Heating and ventilation had to be adapted to the specific situation of the historic building to make it ready for permanent use. The undercroft in the windowless crypt also required a fresh air supply and heating for the new assembly room accommodating 200 persons. This equipment had to work without causing draught and noise. Even higher requirements existed for the large church interior with 2100 seats. Of particular importance, also, were the climatic conditions for the massive masonry structure which required almost constant thermal and air humidity control owing to totally differing uses and varying exterior temperatures during the year. It is important to leave, for instance, wet clothing in a cloakroom outside the church. Especially critical was the humidity coming from visitors who used the cupola ascent before the completion of the building, although special plaster, suitable for various climatic conditions, was used there and ventilation slots along the spiral ramp were inserted. Floor heating was installed as basic heating on the galleries and under the pews on the ground floor. Radiators were added in the window areas (Fig. 186). The first years of using the new building will show if the specifications of the technical equipment were correct or if additional heating areas and other equipment are required.

The planners of the modern electric lighting system for the Frauenkirche had also to find a solution meeting not only the high requirements for the illumination of music performances and TV transmissions but also enabling a lower illumination level and a more intimate atmosphere. All was based on the principle that the artificial illumination had to copy George Bähr's deliberately introduced natural illumination with its intensification towards the choir space and up into the painted cupola. Decisions on lighting should

Fig. 185: Gallery construction using sectional steel

Fig. 186: Installed floor heating in the 2nd gallery

never get out of hand but always serve the historically authentic baroque spatial experience by arranging the lamps as suitably as possible within the interior. The same applied to the acousticians who, in an unobtrusive way, had to install the loudspeakers needed for a good clarity of speech on both choir pillars and on the galleries, as well as the equipment for those with hearing difficulties and the sound studio, as modern accessories in a historic building. According to tradition and from the evidence of first measurements, the near-original interior with its multiple broken and curved shell surfaces promises a unique sound quality.

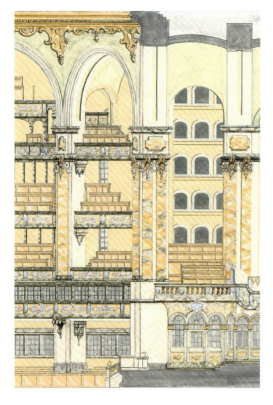

The decision on the colouring of the interior had been left open during rebuilding for a long time. There existed no reliable descriptions or pictures of the original colouring from the time when it was built and the several alterations to the colouring over 200 years had not been well documented. Only on very few pieces of rubble could remains of the succession of different paint layers be analysed and by comparing them with the results obtained by archive research it was possible to come to certain conclusions. It was tempting to leave the impressive stone façade of the unfinished interior on aesthetic grounds, but this in no way corresponded with the perception of baroque architecture and the agreed guidelines for rebuilding. It was necessary to copy carefully the original bright colouring for which some of the baroque churches in Saxony could serve as examples for a possible original tone of colour or for the type of marbling on the pillars and gallery balustrades. The restorer Wolfgang Benndorf drew up a plan for the reconstitution of the baroque polychromy of the church interior (Fig. 187). It was then implemented true to scale in test section F, inspected by a group of experts (Fig. 61), changed and developed further together with the chief restorer Peter Taubert and coordinated with Christoph Wetzel's paintings in the cupola. Wetzel had intensively studied Grone's work, his artistic design and painting technique which allowed him finally to create an enchanting reproduction of the Apostles and the allegoric figures of the Christian virtues which were of the same high standard as the original.

Altogether, the colour design of the church interior can be regarded as a free invention of today's artists in the spirit of the builders in the 18th century; however, the colour traces on the recovered pieces of rubble of the altar were so telling that a historically correct reconstruction of the original colouring could be conceived (Fig. 188). The reconstruction of the architecture of the altar and organ fronts and the figural decorations by stone-restorers was the result of laborious work lasting several years and requiring sculpturing completion and final painting and gilding to regain the expressive harmony of the work. In addition to this, the polychrome appearance of the interior required an intensification of colour and sheen towards the choir area in which the altar front, with the organ crowning it, had always been the spiritual and liturgical highlight. The difficult question was how to preserve the impression of an authentic monument without the traces of destruction impairing the harmony of the work with regard to aesthetics and content. It seems that a reconciliation of the different ideas on how to reach the aim was finally possible after an arduous process of deliberation. Restoration of the original has not been accomplished with such perfection as to let the onlooker forget the history of the infernal destruction in this place of contemplation. The work on the altar showed – as an example for the entire rebuilding work – how easily the desire for technical quality and artistic perfection can gain its own momentum and how fleeting the breath of history is, which the voices from Dresden wanted to be felt.

Fig. 187: Draft for the reconstruction of the baroque colouring, colour sheet by Wolfgang Benndorf

Fig. 188: Colour design of the church interior with galleries and "Bienenkörben" (southeast)

Fig. 189: Organ by Gottfried Silbermann, condition before the destruction

Fig. 190: Altar and organ front, colour sheet by Wolfgang Benndorf, 1997

Similar problems concern the organ. On the one hand was the wish for a complete, as it were archetypal, reconstruction of the old Silbermann organ (Fig. 189), which had been retuned, changed and extended several times during his lifetime and of which, after the destruction, nothing usable remained. The alternative to such a copy was the building of a completely new organ respecting the technical and sound structure of the former Frauenkirche organ but at the same time offering new technical and musical possibilities for playing. After long consideration and discussions the Foundation Council decided in favour of having such a new instrument, which would have to be installed in a reconstructed organ case which was true to the original and in accordance with Bähr's design of the organ front. The order was placed with the Strasbourg workshop of Daniel Kern. This craftsman stands in the tradition of Alsatian organ building and in the succession of Silbermann's sons who had worked there and one gets the impression that he has been successful in achieving the historic Frauenkirche sound as it was intended by Gottfried Silbermann. The new organ front and the sculptured design of the organ gallery had to be created as a free reproduction with the help of old pictures and photographs – without the benefit of dimensions and details of shapes (Fig. 190). In many intermediate stages of developing a model and designing the sculptural decorations, assessment and adjustment and finally creating the colouring and gilding to match the entire area of the choir, an overall work of art has been created which pictorially joins in the jubilating sound of "musica sacra" (Fig. 191).

Fig. 191: Completed organ front with main organ
Installed by Daniel Kern

New life in the Frauenkirche

The rebuilt Frauenkriche is a haven where new life can develop, as described in the Guidelines of the Frauenkirche Foundation in 1994, and as it has been gradually growing in the undercroft over the years of rebuilding. The original designation of this House of God, i. e. for the Lutheran divine service with preaching and Sacrament, was paramount in the considerations of what should go into the rebuilt shell; this could be done in any form compatible with our time and the dignity and beauty of the building. At the same time the future use of the church should take into account the special features of this monument. The Frauenkirche is a place full of meaning for the people of this city and our country, a place of history for the Christian community and public life, a place of memory, remembrance, and reconciliation after the horror of war and destruction, a place of faith and reflexion, meeting and music and – last but not least – a symbol of the wonderful community of people inspired by the same idea and united by this unique rebuilding work.

The new Frauenkirche will probably always be a church without a community in the classic sense but it will have a community of a new type. It will be a church offering something to people and being open to those who have not yet found a Christian community to which they belong, having unanswered questions and looking for a direction in their life. It will concentrate more than usual on the more anonymous, individualist urban way of living, on a temporary and uncommitted interest in what the church is doing and also on the great receptiveness of tourists during their short stay. It will offer opportunities for meeting and dialogue, perhaps even for finding a new community in faith. There will always be a church team who can be asked for information, advice and pastoral care.

Therefore, the Frauenkirche will always be an open church making it easy for everybody to cross the threshold. The access to the viewing platform on top of the cupola is of special attraction for tourists since its completion. There are independent but also general or thematic guided tours possible in the church, e. g. on the paintings in the cupola, the altar, the organ or the church as a place of remembrance and reconciliation. Nearly half a million visitors took part in the guided tours in the undercroft in 2004 and this interest has increased after the consecration of the church. All important information on the building is available in the church and audioguides can be hired for individual tours. Twice a day a short service is offered with a subsequent guided tour in the church – one as a midday service in the form of a service with organ accompaniment and at 6 p.m. as evening prayer in various forms. In the place where the cross, recovered from the heap of rubble, has been posi-

tioned in the interior of the church, people have the opportunity to light candles for the preservation of peace and write a wish for peace in a book. The tradition of prayers for peace in front of the ruin will thus be continued in a different form.

There are two divine services on Sundays as a culmination of the spiritual life in the Frauenkirche. A regular preaching service with liturgy and singing, church music with organ accompaniment and choir is planned for 11 a.m., with can-

Fig. 192: View from the Brühl Terrace over the Münzgasse to the Frauenkirche

Fig. 193: Musical meditation with Ulrich Thiem in the undercroft church

Fig. 194: Chamber choir of the Frauenkirche

tatas being performed on special occasions. The evening services at 6 p.m. will be held in a free form, sometimes as a theme service, in which the preaching is thought of as a "religious talk" on the challenges of our time. Spiritual music is performed on Sunday afternoons every fortnight appropriate to the character of the corresponding Sunday. Holy Communion is celebrated once a month during the main service. Baptisms and marriage ceremonies are possible on certain days. Individual pastoral care is offered at any time and is located in the so-called baptism chapel. A religious seminar will be organized once or twice a year together with the Kreuzkirche for which people should apply and which can result in the baptizing of participants. This offer is based on the religious instruction which was given under the pulpit of the Frauenkirche in the 18th Century or on the memorable biblical instruction by Hugo Hahn during the church's struggle in the Nazi era.

As in former years the Frauenkirche should become a living place for cultivating spiritual music. Famous choirmasters and organists have left lasting traces in the history of Saxon and German music. Both church music posts are today also filled by renowned musicians. Two large choirs and a chamber choir have been brought into being. They perform music in the divine services and the spiritual Sunday music and in addition have their own concerts. Organ concerts take place every Wednesday evening alternating with the Kreuzkirche and the Catholic Cathedral. Organ music at night is planned in June and December as a special offering, with the Frauenkirche being festively illuminated. Performances with Dresden musicians and renowned international ensembles, soloists and choirs have a permanent place in the concert programme of the church as has been the case with the well-received rebuilding concerts in the undercroft. Music performances in the Frauenkirche have their own profile. Special emphasis will thus be placed on special subjects like music of the baroque period or the cultivation of music from Saxony. Musical life in the Frauenkirche is intended to express thoughts of peace and understanding by organizing concerts together with European neighbours and their musical traditions. Besides traditional music it is also possible to continue the "Nachtschwärmer-Meditationen" (night-owl meditations) with jazz music and meditative texts on a specific subject, which have been performed for several years. The series "Literature in the Undercroft" with lectures and readings will also be continued and related to the course of the church year, present-day questions or themes from the Frauenkirche. The manifold possibilities of the new House of God will lead to additional new opportunities for other arts. The undercroft will mainly be a room of tranquillity and remembrance and used only for events on a smaller scale.

The rebuilt church is explicitly to be a centre of efforts for reconciliation and peace, thereby con-

Fig. 195: Divine service in the undercroft church

tinuing the stimulus and warning message of the heap of rubble over recent decades and with a motto for the rebuilding which was visible on the scaffolding from far and wide: "Build bridges – live reconciliation". The recollection of the horrors of war and the guilty involvement of the people in the history of the 20th century, the reconciliation among former enemies and the work for a humane world of peace and justice forms the background of everyday life in the Frauenkirche. This spirit will permanently be present when enjoying the rebuilt House of God and at all events when people come together. It will also be present in the future international youth meetings which in 2001 and 2003 already brought together young people from 12 Dresden twin-towns. It is the basis for cooperation in the international "nail-cross community" with the peace centre in Coventry Cathedral. Last, but not least, the same spirit determines the series of lectures on the subject "Paths to a culture of peace" and the platform discussions pointing out positions and new perspectives on current social questions from a Christian point of view. Aiming especially at young people, i.e. youth groups, school classes and confirmation candidates, the Frauenkirche particularly attempts to be a lively place for understanding history and religion.

The significance of all these new tasks in the Frauenkirche has been expressed by the politician Hans-Jochen Vogel in the following striking words: "The barbarism of a violent regime, the horrors of war and destruction, the will for peace and a new beginning letting the wounds heal but not vanish, the healing understanding of one another and of our former enemies – all this and the will for freedom, for democracy and the unity of the German state within a united Europe is present in this rebuilt House of God to a degree for which it is hard to find an equal. Those asking for the meaning of human life, for direction beyond just the day can find an answer here.
Here the stones speak to all who want to listen".

Sources

The contributions of specialists in the book "The Frauenkirche in Dresden – Inception – Impact – Rebuilding" published by the Frauenkirche Foundation on the occasion of the re-consecration on 30th October 2005, served as the basis for the overall description of the building history and the rebuilding of the Frauenkirche, summarized in the present book.

We should like to thank the Frauenkirche Foundation, the photographer Jörg Schöner and the authors, mentioned below for letting us have the comprehensive material:

Gerhard Glaser, Christoph Münchow, Stefan Herzig, Heinrich Magirius, Torsten Remus, Christoph Wetzel, Karl-Ludwig Hoch, Hans-Christian Hoch, Ludwig Güttler, Eberhard Burger, Wolfram Jäger, Bernd Kluge, Fritz Wenzel, Jörg Peter, Andreas Wycislok, Christoph Frenzel, Uwe Kind, Thomas Gottschlich, Hendrik Heidelmann, Christoph Hein, Wolfgang Benndorf, Horst Hodick, Steffen Heitmann, Bernhard Walter, Stephan Fritz

Further sources acknowledged are:

- 10 yearbooks of the Gesellschaft zur Förderung des Wiederaufbaus der Frauenkirche e.V. and the Stiftung Frauenkirche Dresden from 1995 to 2004
  Verlag Herrmann Böhlaus Nachfolger Weimar

- Exhibition catalogue, George Bähr – Die Frauenkirche und das bürgerliche Bauen in Dresden (The Frauenkirche and civic building in Dresden) 2000
  Staatliche Kunstsammlungen Dresden
  and Landesamt für Denkmalpflege Sachsen

- Dresdner Hefte, No. 32 (4/92) and No. 71 (2nd edition 2/05)
  Dresdner Geschichtsverein e.V.

- Fritz Löffler, Die Frauenkirche zu Dresden – Das Christliche Denkmal (The Dresden Frauenkirche – The Christian Monument) / No. 2, Union Verlag Berlin 1984.

- Fritz Löffler, Das Alte Dresden – Geschichte seiner Bauten (Old Dresden – History of its Buildings),
  E. A. Seemann Verlag Leipzig 1982.

- Hans-Joachim Kuke, Die Frauenkirche in Dresden – „Ein Sankt Peter der wahren evangelischen Religion (The Dresden Frauenkirche – „A Saint Peter of the true Protestant Religion), Wernersche Verlagsgesellschaft Worms 1996.

- Matthias Gretzschel, Die Dresdner Frauenkirche
  Ellert & Richter Verlag Hamburg 1994

- Hans Strehlow / Jens Wonneberger, Der Atem der Steine – Die Ruine der Frauenkirche in Dresden (The breath of the stones – The ruin of the Dresden Frauenkirche
  Verlag Herrmann Schmidt Mainz 1993

Continuing literature

- Frauenkirche Dresden, bibliography 1680–1989 (705 titles) by Rudolf Quaiser
  Frauenkirchen-Jahrbuch 2004, p. 247–288

- Frauenkirche Dresden, bibliography 1990–1996 (188 titles) by Ulrich Voigt
  Frauenkirchen-Jahrbuch 1997, p. 247–262

- Frauenkirche Dresden, bibliography 1997–2000 (306 titles) by Ulrich Voigt
  Frauenkirchen-Jahrbuch 2001, p. 373–398

Illustrations

Jörg Schöner
has followed the progress of the rebuilding of the Frauenkirche with photographs since 1993. More than 4500 photographs were taken during this time, of which about 1000 were selected for this book.

All photographs not mentioned in the list were taken by Jörg Schöner.

- Büro Fritz Wenzel (Karlsruhe)
  Figs. 109, 118
- Büro Heidelmann und Hein (Dresden)
  Figs. 129, 139
- Büro Jäger (Radebeul)
  Fig. 119
- Büro Peter und Lochner (Stuttgart)
  Fig. 117
- Giersch, Steffen (Dresden)
  Figs. 2, 3
- Hoch, Hans-Christian (Dresden)
  Fig. 107
- IPRO
  Figs. 113, 114, 120, 121, 122, 124
- Kunsthalle Düsseldorf
  Fig. 78
- Landeshauptstadt Dresden, Stadtplanungsamt
  Figs. 32, 101, 102, 103, 104, 105
- Landeskirchenamt Sachsen
  Figs. 68, 70, 72
- Leithold, Arthur (Dresden)
  Fig. 73
- Nachlass Georg Rüth
  Fig. 110
- Nadler, Hans (Dresden)
  Figs. 93, 99
- Privatbesitz
  Figs. 8, 74
- Schölzel, Dieter (Dresden)
  Fig. 15
- Sächsische Landes- und Universitätsbibliothek
  Figs. 1, 11, 26, 27, 33, 34, 35, 37, 38, 39, 56, 80, 95, 98, 123, 181
- Sächsisches Landesamt für Denkmalpflege
  Figs. 12, 13, 20, 30, 31, 42, 43, 46, 49, 50, 52, 54, 57, 82, 85, 86, 88, 89, 90, 91, 94, 96, 97, 108, 189
- Sächsisches Landesamt für Denkmalpflege, Torsten Remus
  Figs. 40, 41, 134
- Staatliche Kunstsammlungen Dresden, Alte Meister
  Figs. 53, 81
- Staatliche Kunstsammlungen Dresden, Kupferstich-Kabinett
  Figs. 36, 69, 75, 79
- Staatliche Kunstsammlungen Dresden, Neue Meister
  Figs. 77, 92
- Staatsgalerie Stuttgart
  Fig. 83
- Stadtarchiv Dresden
  Figs. 14, 16, 17, 18, 19, 21, 22, 23, 24, 25, 28, 44, 45, 48, 51, 55, 84
- Stadtmuseum Dresden
  Fig. 47
- Städtische Galerie im Lenbachhaus, München
  Fig. 76
- Stiftung Frauenkirche
  Figs. 187, 190
- Strub, Christine (München)
  Fig. 7
- Thiele, Günther (Dresden)
  Fig. 128

Chronology of the History of the Frauenkirche